The Answer to Bad Religion Is Not No Religion

*A Guide to Good Religion
for Seekers, Skeptics, and Believers*

The Answer to Bad Religion Is Not No Religion

A Guide to Good Religion
for Seekers, Skeptics, and Believers

MARTIN THIELEN

WESTMINSTER
JOHN KNOX PRESS
LOUISVILLE · KENTUCKY

First edition
Published by Westminster John Knox Press
Louisville, Kentucky

14 15 16 17 18 19 20 21 22 23—10 9 8 7 6 5 4 3 2 1

Book design by Drew Stevens
Cover design by designpointinc.com

Library of Congress Cataloging-in-Publication Data
Thielen, Martin, 1956-
   The answer to bad religion is not no religion : a guide to good religion for seekers, skeptics, and believers / Martin Thielen. -- First edition.
      pages cm
   ISBN 978-0-664-23947-3 (alk. paper)
   1. Apologetics--Textbooks. I. Title.
   BT1108.T45 2014
   239--dc23
                                                                2013041192

CONTENTS

PREFACE

Several years ago Jerry and Susan Walker (not their real names) and their two children visited my congregation. Up until that time the Walker family had never attended church. Like many young adults they thought Christianity was judgmental, closed minded, antiscience, and antiwomen. And yet, one Sunday morning, they showed up for worship at First United Methodist Church.

When they returned the following week, I offered to set up a time when I could visit with them. Although polite, they made clear they were just checking us out and not interested in scheduling a visit. The weeks went by and they kept returning each Sunday until, several months later, they scheduled an appointment with me to discuss baptism and church membership. During our visit I asked them, "What first attracted you to our congregation?"

"The sign," they said.

"What sign?" I asked.

"The sign in front of your church that says, 'Open Hearts, Open Minds, and Open Doors.' We thought all churches were narrow-minded and judgmental. So when we saw your sign, we decided to visit. When we discovered the church inside lived up to the sign outside, we wanted to become members."

Before joining our congregation, the Walker family belonged to a subgroup of Americans whom sociologists call the "nones." This term comes from national surveys that ask people to identify their religious preference. In this survey people self-identify as "Protestant," "Catholic," "Jewish," "Muslim," "Buddhist," "Hindu," or "Other." They can also choose "None." So "nones" are people who have no formal religious affiliation. That does not mean they are not interested in spirituality. In fact, many nones describe themselves as "spiritual but not religious." Only a small percentage of them are atheists. For many years only 6 percent of Americans were nones. However, over the past decade that number has skyrocketed. Today 20 percent of the population are nones, and that number is rapidly growing, especially among young adults like the Walkers. One-third of adults age eighteen to twenty-nine currently have no religious affiliation.

What prompted this major increase in religiously unaffiliated people? Researchers have discovered that by the early 1990s most Americans identified Christianity with religious-right fundamentalism. This brand of Christianity is seen by many as arrogant, judgmental, negative, closed-minded, and partisan in its politics. Over the past twenty years, that kind of fundamentalist religion has turned off a huge number of Americans, especially young ones, and caused many of them to reject religion altogether. In essence they said, "If this is Christianity, I want no part of it." This dynamic, say the researchers, is the primary reason for the huge increase in people who now have no religious affiliation.[1]

Like the Walker family, a growing number of Americans are starving for an alternative to negative, closed-minded, judgmental, partisan, antiwomen, antiscience religion. Instead, they are searching for a positive, grace-filled, open-minded, gender-equal faith option. Many of them are finding that in moderate and mainline denominations. They are discovering, like the Walker family did, that the answer to bad religion is not no religion but good religion.

Note

1. For a complete overview of this new religious reality in America, see Robert Putnam and David Campbell, *American Grace: How Religion Divides and United Us* (Chicago: Simon & Schuster, 2010).

INTRODUCTION

ONE PASTOR'S STORY

I vividly recall the day I realized that the religion of my previous denomination no longer worked for me. Like Don McLean's classic rock song "American Pie," I remember "the day the music died." I was a young pastor in my late twenties, attending a national meeting of ministers in my old church. A well-known speaker was preaching. During his sermon he said, "God does not hear the prayer of a Jew." All around me pastors clapped their hands and enthusiastically shouted, "Amen!" and "Preach it, Brother!" His intolerant and hateful words about Jewish believers, combined with the positive response it elicited, literally made me sick to my stomach. I got up from my seat and walked out of the auditorium. In hindsight I probably should have driven home, resigned my church, left my denomination, and never returned. But at that point in my life, I wasn't ready for such a drastic decision. It took another decade to finally arrive at that necessary ending.

I did not grow up in the life of the church. My first real experience with Christianity came at age fifteen. At the time I was a mixed-up young man searching for answers. Through a series of life-changing events, I landed in a conservative church in Muskogee, Oklahoma. At that church I first heard the gospel message, affirmed faith in Christ, was baptized, and fully immersed myself in the life of the congregation. Soon thereafter I felt a call to vocational ministry. After high school I attended a Christian college where I received an excellent education in religion. I had exceptional professors who taught me an open-minded and progressive faith. After a few years of faith struggles and a short but positive career in the insurance business, I went to seminary. Upon graduation I landed at a county seat "First Church" pastorate. That congregation accepted, loved, and affirmed me, giving me a joyful and healthy birth into pastoral ministry.

It's Hard to Leave Your Family

However, during that decade of college, seminary, and my first pastorate, my old denomination began a dramatic shift toward religious-right fundamentalism. I grew increasingly uncomfortable with the toxic direction my denomination was taking. And then I attended the pastors' meeting I just mentioned. Another speaker at that same event said, "Brothers (all the pastors were men), you don't need to seek truth. You already have all the truth you need." Then, holding up his Bible, he said, "You just need to proclaim the truth." I still remember thinking, "If I ever come to a time or place when I stop seeking truth, I hope somebody will put me out of my misery."

So why didn't I leave my church right then? As many people know, it's hard to leave your family, even when it's dysfunctional. Plus, I was young and idealistic. I naively believed that I and other "moderates" in the denomination would eventually win the day. In the end, however, we lost the battle completely.

I also had selfish reasons for staying. I served a large church for my age, with growing opportunities to speak, publish, teach, and serve on various boards and committees. I had a promising future ahead of me. And I was ignorant of the broader Christian community. For example, I had no knowledge of mainline churches. I did not know other places existed in the Christian family where people affirmed more progressive and open-minded faith. I had never even visited a Methodist, Episcopal, or Presbyterian church. My religious worldview was extremely provincial and narrow.

Over the next decade I continued to experience professional opportunities. I published several books with my denomination, wrote dozens of articles, was on the speaking circuit, and pastored tall-steeple churches. And then, at a young age, I was invited to work at the denominational headquarters, working with pastors and music ministers throughout the country in the area of worship and preaching. Although uncomfortable with the direction of my denomination, I loved my work and felt I had too much to lose to seriously consider leaving.

But the drumbeat of religious-right fundamentalism continued to overtake my denomination. Leaders demanded that members believe in biblical inerrancy (everything in the Bible must be interpreted literally), told women they could not serve as clergy and must submit to their husbands, and became intensely partisan in their politics. Large numbers of professors at our seminaries and leaders at our agencies were being fired or forced out for being "liberals." The church that introduced me to Christ, that loved and educated me, and that had given me wonderful opportunities of service was, at least from my perspective, being destroyed. Finally, I came to believe the national leaders of my denomination were guilty of heresy—not doctrinal heresy, but heresy of spirit. Their arrogant, judgmental, mean-spirited, and intolerant positions were the exact opposite of the spirit of Jesus Christ. I could no longer avoid the new realities of my church. I faced a spiritual and vocational crisis.

The Cost of Staying

Sick to my soul over these developments, I scheduled a lunch appointment with an older, wiser, and respected pastor. He, like me, felt devastated over the toxic faith taking over our beloved church. However, with only a few years before his retirement, a denominational change was not a viable option for him. But I was still in my thirties. During lunch I kept talking to my older pastor friend about "the cost of leaving." I moaned about losing my status, my financial compensation level, my publishing and teaching opportunities, and the only church I had ever known. He listened with compassion. But then he said, "Martin, you've been telling me about the cost of leaving. Now I want you to tell me about the cost of *staying*." His question was a burning-bush epiphany for me. I knew at that moment I could no longer stay in my church of origin. The cost of staying—loss of integrity, identifying with a denomination I could no longer affirm, and constant anxiety—was much higher than the cost of leaving. It was time to go.

I want to be clear that I deeply appreciate the many gifts my old denomination gave me. They introduced me to Jesus, loved me, educated me, and gave me exceptional opportunities of service. And I want to affirm that my old church is full of wonderful laypeople and clergy who love

God and serve Jesus faithfully and who are fellow brothers and sisters in Christ. My controversy was not (and is not) with the people in the pews or most of the people in the pulpits. My problem was with the national leaders who, in the name of religious purity, engaged in ruthless ecclesiastical power politics and decimated a beautiful and wonderful religious tradition.

And so, in 1994, I left my old denomination and began a journey that had an uncertain destination and future. For a while I felt absolutely lost. I even considered leaving vocational ministry altogether. But in spite of my wounds and the grief over losing my previous church family, I knew God had called me to serve as a minister of the gospel. A year later, after much soul searching and investigation, I landed in the United Methodist Church, a denomination of "Open Hearts, Open Minds, and Open Doors." In this mainline denomination (which, like every church, has flaws) I felt like I had finally arrived home. For the first time in my life, I experienced an orthodox and centrist faith that was also grace-filled, open-minded, gender-inclusive, tolerant, and life-giving. Through this experience I've learned that the answer to bad religion is not no religion but good religion. To that subject we now turn our attention.

PART 1

THE ANSWER TO BAD RELIGION

Way back in 1859 Charles Darwin startled the world by publishing his famous (many would say infamous) book *On the Origin of Species*, which laid out his theory of evolution. You may know that at the end of his life, Charles Darwin was an atheist. However, that was not always the case. Darwin was raised in the Anglican Church and even considered becoming a clergyman. So, what caused him to renounce Christianity? Many people believe Darwin lost his faith because of his belief in evolution. But that's incorrect. To the end of his life, Darwin insisted that evolution was completely compatible with Christian faith. Neither science nor evolution caused Darwin to reject Christianity. Instead, bad religion caused Darwin to become an atheist. For example, when his beloved daughter died at the age of ten, Darwin blamed God. Eventually he quit believing in God altogether. He simply could not believe in a God that killed off ten-year-old children. I don't blame him. I don't believe in that kind of God either. If space permitted, I could give you other examples of how bad theology under-mined Darwin's faith, including the doctrine that all Jews were destined for a devil's hell. In the end it wasn't science but bad religion that caused Darwin's atheism.

Unfortunately, there continues to be a lot of bad religion out there, still causing people to lose their faith. Though this book focuses on Protestant Christianity, bad religion affects other traditions as well. For example, think of all those young Muslim men and women who blow themselves up, along with dozens of innocent people—all in the name of God. Think about all those Roman Catholic priests who molested children and all the bishops who covered it up. There's plenty of bad religion in Protestant churches, too. I recently heard about a Baptist preacher from California who prays daily, in the name of Jesus, for God to kill President Obama. Sadly I could go on and on. Bad religion abounds, including closed-minded religion, arrogant religion, intolerant religion, and judgmental religion. You can add to that list religion that tells women they are inferior to men and religion that says science is the enemy of faith. When I think of all the bad religion out there, especially in the Christian faith, I can relate to the musician Bono's statement, "Christians are hard to tolerate. I don't know how Jesus does it."

In the pages that follow, we review a few examples of bad religion, primarily focused on Protestant Christianity in the United States. This list is not anywhere near comprehensive, and not everyone will agree that these examples constitute unhealthy religion. But they are illustrative of the kind of religion that turns many people away from Christian faith.

1

BAD RELIGION ENGAGES IN SELF-RIGHTEOUS JUDGMENT OF OTHERS

On Mother's Day 2012, a North Carolina Baptist pastor preached a disturbing sermon that went viral. In his sermon this pastor said, "I figured a way to get rid of all the lesbians and queers. Build a great big large fence, fifty or a hundred miles long, put all the lesbians in there. Fly over and drop some food. Do the same thing with the queers and the homosexuals and have that fence electrified so they can't get out. And you know what? In a few years, they'll die out. Do you know why? They can't reproduce!" He later added, "It makes me pukin' sick to think about. Can you imagine kissing some man?"

Whatever you think about homosexuality, this kind of hateful condemnation is deeply troubling. It's also a prime example of bad religion. And it's not a new development. Even in Jesus' day, judgmental religion was a serious problem. Many passages of Scripture reveal it, including the parable of the Pharisee and the Tax Collector praying at the temple in Luke 18:9–14. The story begins, "To some who were confident of their own righteousness and looked down on everyone else, Jesus told this parable" (Luke 18:9). In the parable the Pharisee thanked God that he was not a terrible sinner like the tax collector praying on the other side of the temple. Meanwhile the tax collector prayed for God to be merciful to him, a sinner. At the end of the story, Jesus affirmed the contrite tax collector and criticized the self-righteous, judgmental Pharisee. Throughout his ministry Jesus regularly challenged the arrogant and judgmental religion he saw all around him.

Before diving into the topic of judging, I need to make an important clarification. When Jesus said, "Do not judge," he was not saying we should never evaluate a person's character. Jesus' command not to judge people doesn't mean we overlook lying, cheating, stealing, or criminal behavior. Jesus is not saying we never hold people accountable for their behavior. What Jesus is saying is that having a self-righteous, superior, judgmental, condemning attitude toward others is bad religion, and we need to avoid it.

One of the most famous biblical stories dealing with judgmental religion is found in John 8:1–11. A woman is caught in the act of adultery. Religious leaders wanted to stone her to death in accord with Jewish law. Jesus responded, "Let any one of you who is without sin be the first to throw a stone at her" (John 8:7). Eventually everyone left the scene, leaving their stones behind. This powerful story of grace illustrates at least four problems with judgmental religion.

1. *Judging is selective.* The story begins like this. "The teachers of the law and the Pharisees brought in a woman caught in adultery. They made her stand before the group and said to Jesus, 'Teacher, this woman was caught in the act of adultery'" (John 8:3–4). Even a quick review of the story reveals a major problem. The man involved in this adulterous affair was missing! The religious leaders were

quick to judge, but their judging was selective. They condemned the woman but not the man. Modern-day judging is the same. We come down hard on some people but not others. We condemn some sins but ignore other sins. For example, a few years ago a pastor in middle Tennessee said in a sermon, "Homosexuals will not be allowed into heaven." That comment is troubling on many levels. First, God makes the decision who makes it into heaven and who doesn't, not preachers. Second, there's no doubt his comment caused a lot of pain for people in that congregation who were gay or had loved ones who were gay. But mostly this story is an example of selective judging. The pastor supported his pronouncement with several passages of Scripture—texts that Christian believers interpret differently.[1] But the same passages this pastor used to condemn homosexual behavior also speak about pride, greed, lust, adultery, gossip, gluttony, and dishonoring parents. That preacher didn't say prideful people won't be allowed into heaven. He didn't say gluttons won't be allowed into heaven. He didn't say gossips won't be allowed into heaven, or greedy people, or lustful people, or children who disrespect their parents. He only said homosexuals won't make it into heaven. One of the major problems with judging is that it is selective. We are quick to judge other people's sins, but not our own.

2. *Judging is destructive.* In this story religious leaders said to Jesus, "'In the Law Moses commanded us to stone such women. Now what do you say?' They were using this question as a trap, in order to have a basis for accusing him" (John 8:5–6). As we see in this text, judging others is destructive. Obviously, the judging in this story would have been destructive for this woman. If the religious leaders had carried out their plan, she would have been executed in a brutal fashion. But that's not the only destructiveness we see here. The scribes and Pharisees were also trying

to destroy Jesus. They used this episode to trap Jesus, to have ammunition against him. They were hoping he would say, "No, don't stone her," so that they could accuse him of not believing the Bible and not obeying the law of Moses. The entire episode was terribly destructive. Arrogant, self-righteous judging always hurts people.

We see that clearly in America today. Hateful judgment of others is epidemic in our country and is polarizing us in dangerous ways. That's especially true in politics. For example, during the last election cycle, I heard a person on the political right call people on the political left "a bunch of communists." Think about that. Should we really be calling people "communists"? Communism as practiced under brutal dictators like Stalin and Mao was responsible for the slaughter of millions of people in the twentieth century. In fact, it just about destroyed the world. We need to think twice before we accuse someone of being a communist. But don't think I'm picking on the political right because it's no better on the left. A week later I heard a person on the political left call people on the political right "the American Taliban." Do you really think we should be calling people "the Taliban"? The Taliban indiscriminately blow people up with bombs, behead people, throw acid on women's faces, and burn down schools. This kind of hateful judgment, on both the left and the right, is tearing our country apart. It's destructive. And it is inappropriate for Christian believers.

But judging isn't just destructive on a national level. Judging is also destructive on a personal level. When we judge people, we—at least partially—destroy them. I once heard a story by Tony Campolo that broke my heart. During his school years Tony knew a boy whose classmates constantly picked on him. He was different from the other boys, sort of effeminate, so during junior high school some of the students began calling him a sissy. By high school they suspected he was a homosexual, and their judgment got worse. They called him "homo, fag, queer," and worse. They were merciless in their judgment of this boy. Then one day, right after gym class, five boys cornered him in the locker room shower and urinated on him. Afterward they walked off laughing. He showered again, dressed, and made it through the rest of the day. But the damage had been done; the breaking point had arrived. That night he hung himself in the basement of his house. This young man made a horrible decision to kill himself. But when we judge and condemn others, we hurt them, we tear them down, we break their spirit, and sometimes we literally destroy them. Self-righteous judging of others is always destructive.

3. *Judging is hypocritical.* The story in John 8 continues, "When they kept on questioning him, he straightened up and said to them, 'Let any one of you who is without sin be the first to throw a stone at her.' Again he stooped down and wrote on the ground. At this, those who heard began to go away one at a time, the older ones first, until only Jesus was left, with the woman still standing there" (John 8:7–9). The point here is clear: We have no business judging the sins of others when we have sins of our own. Unless we are perfect, when we judge others, we are hypocrites. Only perfect people have the right to judge others. And there are no perfect people.

This story reminds me of the time when former President Bill Clinton engaged in sexual misconduct with a young intern named Monica Lewinsky. Lest I be misunderstood, I believe Bill Clinton's behavior in this matter was despicable. I was highly disappointed in his actions and am not defending him. But that incident is a vivid example of the hypocrisy of judging others. When the news broke about Clinton's affair, a lot of people who began casting stones at the president had no business doing so. For example,

Representative Dan Burton called Clinton a "scumbag." Soon thereafter Burton admitted fathering a child outside of marriage. Senator Steven Johnson also attacked Clinton for his misbehavior; Johnson, a married man, later admitted to having a sexual affair with a twenty-three-year-old intern who worked in his office, just one year before Clinton's affair. Representative Helen Chenoweth, a prominent critic of Clinton's sexual conduct, later conceded she had carried on a six-year extramarital affair herself. Representative Henry Hyde, who viciously attacked Clinton's sexual sins, fessed up that in his forties he carried on an extramarital fling with a married woman, although he discounted it as a "youthful indiscretion." The whole incident was a pitiful spectacle of pure hypocrisy. We had all these senators and representatives throwing stones at the president for having an affair while they were guilty of affairs of their own. Unless we are perfect, when we judge others, we are being hypocritical. That's why Jesus said, "Let any one of you who is without sin be the first to throw a stone at her" (John 8:7).

4. *Judging violates the example and teaching of Jesus.* The story concludes, "Jesus straightened up and asked her, 'Woman, where are they? Has no one condemned you?' 'No one, sir,' she said. 'Then neither do I condemn you,' Jesus declared. 'Go now and leave your life of sin'" (John 8:10–11). One final reason for not judging others is that judging violates the example and teaching of Christ. Jesus was the only person in the world who had the right to condemn this woman, but he did not do so. That does not mean Jesus was soft on sin. In fact, Jesus told this woman to go and sin no more. Jesus did not condone her behavior. Jesus did throw out one of the Ten Commandments that says, "You shall not commit adultery" (Exod. 20:14). But neither did he condemn her. Jesus knew people need grace, not judgment. In this text and in many other passages in

the Bible, Jesus tells us not to judge others. When we do judge, we violate the example and the teaching of our Lord. For the four reasons mentioned above, self-righteous judgment of others is bad religion and needs to be discarded.

Note

1. For an overview of the three major Christian positions on homosexuality, see chapter 9 of my book *What's the Least I Can Believe and Still Be a Christian: A Guide to What Matters Most* (Louisville, KY: Westminster John Knox Press, 2011).

2

BAD RELIGION EXPRESSES
A CHRONIC SPIRIT
OF NEGATIVITY

The federal government once employed a veterinarian as a food inspector. He inspected seventy-five thousand chickens a week at a local poultry company. One day he made an interesting comment to a friend. He said, "I never see a good chicken." He went on to explain that through years of inspecting millions of chickens, it became necessary for him to train his eyes to see only the bad chickens, the ones that should be rejected.

Unfortunately, religious people can sometimes become like that chicken inspector. They focus only on the negatives. They are known for what they are against rather than what they are for. They are against gambling. They are against drinking. They are against gays. They are against women's rights. They are against the teachings of science such as evolution or global warming. They are against Muslims. Eventually, their spirit of negativism erases joy, grace, and beauty in their life. Their religion becomes a religion of negativity.

A Downcast Spirit Dries Up the Bones

About a year ago, after one of our weekend services, a young man walked up to me and said he was a "nondenominational, independent fundamentalist Christian." He said he had heard positive things about our church and decided to visit. Then, with a scowl on his face, he said, "Your church is dead and unfaithful to God, just like every other mainline denominational church in America." As he angrily walked away, he said loudly, "This is not a true church."

It was a sad scene. During the worship service he had just visited, our new orchestra played beautifully. The choir sang an inspiring anthem. We baptized a child. Two young adults reaffirmed their faith and joined our congregation. And we showed a brief video about our partnership with an organization that trains youth ministers all over America and beyond. But he saw none of these positive, life-giving elements. Instead, he saw everything through the lens of radical negativity. His demeanor and words reminded me of Proverbs 17:22, which says, "A cheerful heart is a good medicine, but a downcast spirit dries up the bones" (NRSV). Negative religion indeed dries up the bones of life and joy and is a far cry from the spirit of Jesus who said that he came so that we might have abundant life.

Unfortunately, the spirit of religious negativism expressed by our guest at worship that Sunday is not unusual. For example, several months after my last book was published, an unhappy reader sent me a long letter. In his letter, the author made many references to my book and responded with statements such as the following:

> Read your Bible. There's no ambiguity here. Homosexuals are an abomination to the Lord and you should not pretend otherwise. . . . In spite of your words to the

contrary, Islam is a political ideology masquerading as a religion and all Muslims will spend eternity in everlasting punishment in a devil's hell. . . . Global warming is a man-made myth and you are a liar for affirming it. . . . Evolution is a lie from the devil, so how dare you say Christians can believe in it! . . . In spite of what you say in your book, God forbids women to serve as pastors and commands wives to submit to their husbands — case closed.

On and on the letter went. He vented his bitterness and rage in virtually every sentence. Finally, the letter ended by saying, "Your book is going to send a bunch of people to hell—you included."

In my younger years, such a letter would have made me feel defensive and angry. But at this point in my life, the letter mostly made me feel sad that a person—in the name of Jesus Christ and Christianity—could be so overwhelmingly hostile and negative. Such is the spirit of unhealthy religion.

I'm certainly not saying that religion should always be happy and easygoing. Sometimes a hard prophetic word needs to be made. Pain and suffering need to be acknowledged and responded to. Sin is real. There is a cross at the center of Christianity. Jesus wept. But a constant negative and critical spirit is not the spirit of healthy faith. At heart, faith is about love, hope, joy, peace, gratitude, and wonder. Chronic negativism is an enemy to true faith.

They Conspired to Destroy Him

Unfortunately, negative religion was highly prevalent during the time of Jesus. For example, the New Testament includes many stories of Jesus healing people on the Sabbath. Instead of responding in awe, joy, and celebration for the healings, many religious leaders responded with rage that Jesus had broken the Jewish law against working on the Sabbath. A vivid example can be found in Mark 3:1–7. In this passage Jesus healed a man with a withered hand at a synagogue on the Sabbath, deeply upsetting religious leaders who were more concerned about a petty legalistic law than the pain and disability of a beloved child of God. Aware of their attitude, the passage says that Jesus "looked around at them in anger" and was "deeply distressed at their stubborn hearts" (v. 5). Chronically negative religion deeply troubled Jesus and even made him angry. After Jesus healed the man with the withered hand, we read, "The Pharisees went out and immediately conspired with the Herodians against him, how to destroy him" (v. 6 NRSV).

Sadly, this kind of negative, legalistic, and joyless religion still abounds today. You can find it among some followers of Islam who reject music, dancing, and art. You can find it among some Jewish groups who foster hatred against all Palestinians and among some Muslim groups who foster hatred against all Jews. You can find it among some religious-right Christian fundamentalists who constantly condemn liberals, science, and modernism. This kind of negative religion eventually drains people of zest, joy, hope, and love, leaving only bitterness in their hearts.

Years ago I served a church that put on an annual mission fair. The fair raised many thousands of dollars for work among the poor in Mexico and Guatemala. One year at the fair, we featured a talented couple who sang numerous country and pop songs. During the concert two men from a neighboring fundamentalist church showed up. They complained about the couple's secular music selections, calling the songs "the devil's music." They caused a major scene at the fair, shouting and condemning the couple and those listening to their music. Finally I had to request that they leave. As they departed, they shouted at the top of their lungs that our church was "an abomination to God" and that we would "all burn in the fire of hell." As they drove off, a member of my congregation said to me, "It's tragic that people can be so negative and hateful in the name of religion."

Let's Kill It

I once heard a story about a little boy who ran into his house one afternoon in near hysteria. He announced to his mom that his pet turtle had rolled over and died. He was inconsolable. When his father came home, he gathered up the tearful boy in his arms. As they sat in front of the dead turtle, the father suggested they could have a funeral for the turtle. Everyone could wear black, there would be a processional, and they could read from the Bible, just like a real funeral. Not only that, the father added, they could bury the turtle in the little tin box they kept the candy in. At this point the boy stopped crying and listened intently. "Then," chimed in the mother, "we can have a party afterward. Wouldn't that be nice?" The boy smiled.

Encouraged, the father went on, "Yes, and we'll have your friends over for the funeral, and we can even have ice cream at the party after the funeral." By now the boy was grinning from ear to ear. But then, suddenly, to the surprise of everyone, the turtle rolled back on his legs and began slowly moving away. The boy looked startled and then exclaimed, "Oh, Daddy, let's kill it."

Negative religion kills joy and grace and love. It's bad religion, and we need to reject it.

3

BAD RELIGION BREEDS ARROGANCE, INTOLERANCE, AND ABSOLUTISM

Several months ago I spoke at a weekend conference in eastern Tennessee. Participants included youth and adults of all ages. During one of my talks, I spoke about the diversity of thought in my congregation from politics, to social issues, to theological beliefs. For example, I noted that people in my congregation had different and even conflicting theological views on homosexuality, the spiritual fate of Muslims, evolution, and abortion. However, I noted that in spite of our diversity we were one body, united in our common faith in Christ, which transcended our differences.

After the session was over, three teenagers from a religious-right church confronted me, obviously angry. They were appalled that a church could have differences of opinion on important doctrines. They said theological diversity on such issues was evil and unacceptable, that God's Word on these subjects was absolute with no room for ambiguity. They accused me of blasphemy and my church of apostasy. It was an incredibly sad experience. I've heard such talk before from adults. But I didn't expect to hear it from high school students.

The Opposite of Faith
Is Not Doubt but Certainty

I hold many strong beliefs about the life, death, and resurrection of Jesus Christ; the love of God; and other crucial Christian affirmations. But when religious people are uncompromisingly absolute about all their beliefs, when they cannot see beyond black-and-white, especially on secondary issues, they are practicing unhealthy religion. The fact is, we are not God. We do not know everything. For example, we don't know how and when God will end the world. We can't fully explain the Trinity. We don't know all the details of Christ's resurrection or our own eternal life. We can't be certain about the spiritual status of people who profess religions other than Christianity. The list goes on and on. Therefore, absolutist religion that has no room for uncertainty and ambiguity is bad religion. As one wise believer once said, "The opposite of faith is not doubt but certainty."

Unfortunately, a lot of Christians have problems accepting ambiguity. They want their belief system to be certain, beyond question; and they often punish those who disagree with their pronouncements. Not long ago I heard an amusing story about a monastery. One of the monks died, and they placed him in the large crypt where they buried all the dead monks. Three days later the monks heard noises coming from inside the crypt. When they removed the stone wall, they found their brother alive. Full of wonderment he said, "Oh brothers, I've been there. I've been to the other side. I've seen heaven!" Then he added,

"And it's nothing like what we've been taught. It's not at all the way our theology says it is!" When he said those words, the other monks threw him back in the crypt and sealed the wall.

Although I chuckled at that story, there is much truth in it. For example, I recently corresponded with a person who wants an absolutist faith, including a perfect and literal Bible devoid of human input or historical nuances of context, including the status of women. This person, extremely unhappy with comments in my previous book affirming equality between husbands and wives and affirmation of women clergy, said, "To me, there is not an in-between. There is either Christianity or there isn't. One either accepts the Bible for what it says or dumps it. Is there a way to reinterpret 2 plus 2 equals 4 on the context of when and where it was written?" This person wanted faith to be absolute, with no uncertainties and no ambiguities, like a mathematical formula. But that kind of faith is not possible and not healthy. As Leonard Sweet said in his book *Viral*, "The true enemy of faith is certainty. The just shall live by faith, not certainty."[1]

One of the many problems with arrogant and closed-minded, absolutist religion is that it makes people intolerant of anyone who disagrees with their rigid positions. For example, years ago a young family began visiting my church. They came from a denomination that taught they were the only true church. When their pastor heard about their visits to my congregation, he went to see them. He told them my church was a "tool of the devil." When they told him they planned to become members of our congregation, he said, "If you do so, you will condemn your children to eternal hell fire and damnation." At that point they asked him to leave their home, and they joined my church the next Sunday. The following Sunday he publicly condemned them during his church worship service and told the members to have no further contact with them. As sad as that story is, absolutist religion can become even more toxic.

Toxic Faith

That was true for a man named Brad Hirschfield, an Orthodox Jew from Chicago. Over time Brad became a religious extremist, convinced his way to God was the only way. He moved to the West Bank in Israel and embraced a fiery political Judaism. Packing a Bible in one hand and a 9mm pistol in the other, he joined a group of radical Jews at a settlement in the West Bank. They believed their religion alone was pure and that their Muslim Palestinian neighbor's religion was evil. One day Brad and his militant buddies got into a firefight with a group of Palestinians. During the fight several of his friends began randomly shooting into a school and killed two innocent Palestinian children. That event changed Brad's life forever. He became physically ill on the spot, nauseous at what he had become—a radical, arrogant, intolerant, religious fanatic. Since that day he has dedicated his life to challenging self-righteous, absolutist, black-and-white, arrogant religion that believes it is superior to others. He wrote a book about his experience called *You Don't Have to Be Wrong for Me to Be Right: Finding Faith without Fanaticism.* Thankfully, Brad now affirms religious humility. He abandoned arrogant religion for a more loving, grace-filled, and tolerant religion.

Arrogant and intolerant absolutist religion is not the spirit of Jesus and is not a part of healthy faith. That's why Jesus taught his followers to reject arrogant religion and be humble in our approach to faith. The fact is, none of us have all the answers. None of us understand everything about God. Just as we cannot fully describe a beautiful painting or a moving symphony, we cannot fully describe and understand God.

A few months ago I watched again the old movie *Children of a Lesser God*. The film tells the story of a man who teaches deaf children and who falls in love with a deaf woman. In one scene the man listened to a record of classical music, one of the great joys of his life. The deaf woman asked him to describe how music sounds. In sign language and interpretative movements he tried his best but finally gave up and said, "I cannot." It's impossible to say in words and signs how music sounds. And it is impossible to say in words or images exactly what God is like.

God is too big to be fully described. We cannot put God in a box and say now we fully understand God and have God all figured out. God cannot be trapped and limited in our theological doctrines, as good as they might be. God is too big, too mysterious, too transcendent, and too glorious to be fully comprehended. As the theologian Rudolf Otto once said, God is the "Mysterium Tremendum, the most unfathomable mystery of all." Our understanding of God and faith can never be completely black-and-white. Instead, some degree of ambiguity and uncertainty is always present. Therefore, absolutist religion is not a part of authentic faith, and we should do all we can to rid ourselves of that kind of attitude.

Seeing through a Glass, Darkly

The apostle Paul understood ambiguity. In 1 Corinthians 13:12 he said, "Now we see but only a reflection as in a mirror." Other translations say, "We see through a glass, darkly." The image here is either looking out a window or else looking into a mirror, and the view is distorted; you can't see clearly. Paul is saying we don't always see things with perfect clarity, we don't always understand everything, and we live with a lot of uncertainty and ambiguity. To make his point further, Paul wrote, "Now I know in part" (v. 12). Incomplete knowledge, understanding, and clarity are the nature of life and faith, especially on complex issues.

Take, for example, the controversial issue of abortion. Some people today see this issue in absolute, black-and-white terms, with no room for question or ambiguity. They say abortion is always wrong, regardless of the circumstances. I used to hold this position, and even today I have severe problems with abortion. I wish we lived in a world where abortion never occurred. In fact, I hate abortion. But I had an experience once that brought my absolute, black-and-white certainty into question. Years ago, when I was a young pastor, a couple in my congregation came to see me. They had just learned that their unborn baby had a horrible genetic disease. If the baby was born and if it lived, the baby would have severe mental and physical disabilities. If it managed to live, the baby would spend months in the intensive care unit, attached to most every machine you could imagine. If the baby survived the first few months, it would then suffer until it died, which virtually always occurred by age two, after a long and difficult struggle. So this couple asked me, "Should we consider an abortion? Given all the circumstances, might that be the best loving and Christian option? Or should we have the baby and do all we can to keep it alive? What do you think is the right and Christian thing to do?" I didn't have an answer. I still don't. Sometimes life and faith are gray and ambiguous. To say otherwise is not true to human experience and is unhealthy religion.

However, to say that absolutist religion is bad religion doesn't mean we grope around in darkness without solid ground on which to stand. Even in 1 Corinthians 13, where

Paul admitted that "we see in a mirror, darkly" and "know only in part," he also said that God has given us the gifts of faith, hope, and love, which are more than enough to guide us through life.

Note

1. Leonard Sweet, *Viral* (Colorado Springs: Waterbrook Press, 2012), 125.

4

BAD RELIGION PARTICIPATES IN PARTISAN POLITICS AND EXCESSIVE NATIONALISM

I once heard a prominent national religious leader say, "I don't know how people can call themselves Christian and still be Democrats." His statement deeply offended me. And I would have been just as offended if he had said, "I don't know how people can call themselves Christian and still be Republicans." Partisan religion, left or right, is inappropriate and unhealthy and has no place in the church of Jesus Christ, for at least five reasons:

1. Partisan politics in the church is illegal.
2. Partisan politics divides congregations.
3. Partisan politics diverts the church from its primary tasks.
4. Partisan politics damages the integrity of the church.
5. Partisan politics politicizes God.

When churches engage in partisan politics, they are engaging in bad religion. While the church should indeed grapple with social issues, engaging in partisan politics by supporting or condemning a particular political candidate or party is out of bounds.

Loss of Perspective

One of the great dangers of partisan religion is that it causes Christians to lose their prophetic perspective, both on the right and on the left. For example, in the run-up to the second Iraq war, virtually every Christian denomination in the world, Catholic and Protestant — including leaders of my own denomination — agreed that a war with Iraq did not meet the historic Christian criteria of a just war and pleaded with then President George W. Bush not to attack Iraq. The only significant exception to this overwhelming consensus against the war was among conservative evangelical churches. In his provocative book, *Bad Religion*, Ross Douthat suggests that religious-right churches were so closely identified with President Bush and the Republican Party that they lost their prophetic perspective and thus fell in line with the invasion of Iraq. This stance, argues Douthat, is a vivid example of bad religion.[1]

However, the same problem can be found among the religious left. Just as religious-right churches tend to identify with the Republican Party, religious-left churches tend to identify with the Democratic Party. One example is that liberal churches, along with many Democrats, often resist any kind of entitlement reform. Yes, the Bible teaches us to care for the poor. But Scripture also calls for fiscal responsibility, including avoiding debt. And the Bible teaches that people need to take personal responsibility for their own life. The apostle Paul once said, "The one who is unwilling to work shall not eat" (2 Thess. 3:10). However, religious-left churches tend to be so closely identified with the Democratic Party that they often resist the message of fiscal responsibility and personal responsibility when it comes to government entitlement programs.

I realize the Iraq War and entitlement reform are complex issues with no simplistic analysis. I'm simply using these two examples to illustrate the danger of partisan religion. When the church is too closely identified with a political party, it can easily cloud our judgment. And sadly, the costs can be tragic, as was the case in Nazi Germany and apartheid South Africa. Therefore, Christians must resist partisan religion at all costs.

"I Am an American First and a Christian Second"

Closely related to partisan politics, and equally inappropriate, is for religion to become extremely nationalistic. Please do not misunderstand. Patriotism is not wrong. However, when it becomes excessive, it qualifies as bad religion.

Years ago, when I graduated from seminary and served my first pastorate, I preached a sermon on Christian citizenship. I told my congregation that I loved my country. I explained that my father served as an air force pilot his entire career. I expressed deep pride in and love for America, but I also noted that patriotism was secondary to Christian faith. Our first priority must always be God, not country. As Isaiah once said, "Surely the nations are like a drop in a bucket; they are regarded as dust on the scales" (Isa. 40:15). After the service a member of the congregation took exception to my sermon. He said, "I am an American first and a Christian second." The problem with that statement is that if we are Americans first and Christians second, we are not Christians. To be Christian means our ultimate allegiance is to God, not country. We can love God and country but always in that order. The two are not equal.

A few years ago I found myself sick on the weekend of July 4. So I stayed home from church that day. I decided to turn on the TV and watch a worship service. I came upon a service from a middle Tennessee nondenominational megachurch. I could barely believe my eyes. The altar had been removed, and in its place sat an army truck. The service began with four military servicemen, one from each branch of the military, rappelling from the roof of the church in full military uniform. A military color guard marched down the aisle with a huge American flag. The pastor preached on God and America and made it sound like being a good American and being a good Christian were one and the same. All the songs were about America, not Jesus. The entire service deeply disturbed me. Excessive nationalism that equates Christianity with America is bad religion and must be rejected.

Church-State Principles

The primary point of this first section is to give examples of bad religion, with partisan politics and excessive nationalism being vivid illustrations. However, while we are on the topic of religion and politics, it seems appropriate to lay out some guidelines for a proper relationship between church and state. The following six biblical principles serve as a starting point.

1. *Christians should respect the government.* As Romans 13:1 says, "Let everyone be subject to the governing authorities, for there is no authority except that which God has established. The authorities that exist have been established by God." God knows that nations need some form

of civil government to function. So Christians are expected to respect their government.

2. *Christians should obey the government (with limits).* Overall, Christians are commanded by God to obey the laws of the land. As we read in Titus 3:1, "Remind the people to be subject to rulers and authorities, to be obedient." However, there are limits to that obedience. If our government tells us to do something contrary to God's law, then civil disobedience is appropriate. We see that in Acts 5:29. In this story Peter and the apostles were commanded by the authorities to stop preaching Jesus. Peter replied, "We must obey God rather than human beings!" As much as possible, Christians should respect and obey their government. But we must always remember that our ultimate allegiance is to God, not the government.

3. *Christians should pray for government leaders.* First Timothy 2:1–2 says, "I urge, then, first of all, that petitions, prayers, intercession and thanksgiving be made for all people—for kings and all those in authority, that we may live peaceful and quiet lives in all godliness and holiness." God expects us to pray for those in authority. For example, God expects us to pray for our president. We may love the president or loathe the president, but either way we are expected to pray for him or her, as well as other national and local leaders.

4. *Christians should pay our share of taxes.* When Jesus was asked if believers should pay taxes, he said, "Give back to Caesar what is Caesar's, and to God what is God's" (Matt. 22:21). In Romans 13:6 we read, "This is also why you pay taxes, for the authorities are God's servants." We may not like giving our money to the IRS, but God expects us to pay our fair share of taxes.

5. *Christians should critique government actions and policies.* Sometimes the government gets it wrong. When that happens, the church is called to critique and even challenge

the decisions of our government. We see this over and over again in the prophets. When national leaders were involved in unjust actions, the prophets spoke out. For example, when the government of Israel catered to the rich at the expense of the poor, God's prophets pounded them. The prophet Micah once said to the rulers of Israel, "Hear this, you leaders of Jacob, you rulers of Israel, who despise justice and distort all that is right; who build Zion with bloodshed, and Jerusalem with wickedness. Her leaders judge for a bribe" (Mic. 3:9–11). Sometimes, the church must speak out against unjust policies of the government. History is full of examples. It was the church, at least part of the church, that challenged the evils of slavery. It was the church, at least part of the church, that challenged unjust racial discrimination laws and led the civil rights movement. It's not easy, but the church must, from time to time, provide a prophetic critique of the state. We explore this further in part 3.

6. *Christians should influence public policy.* The church is never called to rule the government, but we are called to be a positive influence on public policy. As Jesus said in Matthew 5:13–14, "You are the salt of the earth. . . . You are the light of the world." Christians and churches across the land are called by God to be salt and light. We are called to lift up and promote high standards of ethics and integrity. We are called to defend the weak and vulnerable. We are called to promote morality, both private and public. History is full of examples. You might be interested to know that the church helped women get the right to vote. The church influenced our government to pass child labor laws. I could give many other examples. God calls Christians and churches to be a positive influence in public life. And we are also called to help shape public leaders. Almost every president, congressman, senator, Supreme Court

justice, and governor is a member of a faith community. So part of our job is to help instill high values and ethics in both current and future public leaders so that when they take office, they will be leaders of integrity.

Note

1. Ross Douthat, *Bad Religion: How We Became a Nation of Heretics* (Washington, DC: Free Press, 2012), 141.

5

◇◇◇◇◇

BAD RELIGION FOSTERS NOMINAL COMMITMENT TO CHRIST AND CHURCH

Throughout the New Testament, Jesus called on his followers to take their faith seriously. He once told his disciples, "Whoever wants to be my disciple must deny themselves and take up their cross daily and follow me" (Luke 9:23). Near the end of the Sermon on the Mount (Matt. 5–7), Jesus warned his followers against having casual, nominal, halfhearted faith. For example, he said, "Enter through the narrow gate" (7:13). "By their fruit you will recognize them" (7:20). And, "Not everyone who says to me, 'Lord, Lord,' will enter the kingdom of heaven, but only the one who does the will of my Father who is in heaven" (7:21).

In these and many other passages, Jesus calls us to serious commitment to God. Unfortunately, American Christians don't do a good job on that front. Instead, we tend to be nominal and casual about our faith, especially those of us in mainline denominations. Take worship attendance, for example. Obviously, there is far more to being a Christian than attending worship services. On the other hand, weekly worship is a crucial part of following Christ. God deserves our worship. We need to worship. And our church needs us to worship. You can't live out authentic Christian faith without regular congregational worship. Unfortunately, worship attendance figures among American Christians are dismal. Several studies have revealed that less than 25 percent of American church members bother to show up on any given Sunday.

"We Just Love Our Church"

I came across a letter recently that a pastor received from a family in his congregation. The family had not attended worship in several months, so he wrote them a letter saying he missed seeing them at worship. About a week later, he received the following letter from the family:

Dear Pastor,

Thank you for your kind letter. And, yes, we haven't been in church for several months now, so maybe we should explain. In the summer, we go to the lake every weekend. Our kids are young now, and it's so important that they learn how to water-ski and become expert skiers. And we like to get away too, Jack and me, because there's so much going on in our lives and we just need a break. But then when summer's over, soccer begins and our kids all play in the most competitive leagues. They have games every weekend, and sometimes the games are out of town, and when they are in town, we go to the soccer games either on Saturday or Sunday, and there is just no way we can make it to church. We will be back to church. Don't give up on us. There's a brief period of time when soccer is over, and basketball hasn't yet begun, and it's too cold to go to the lake, and that's a great time for us go to church. But then again, it's Christmas, and you know how hectic that is. And after Christmas we just have to go to Colorado to ski, so that time's got a problem too. But one of these days, don't be surprised when you look up and see us out there in the congregation, because we just love you, and we just love our church.

I laughed when I read that but in a painful way. Commitment to God and church among many American Christians is not what it should be. In fact, many people are more committed to their civic groups than to their church. For example, when I joined the Rotary Club years ago, I was told that I had to pay my dues and attend at least 60 percent of the meetings. That got me to thinking, "What if our church had the same requirement? What if everyone in the church had to pay their dues (tithe their income) and attend worship at least 60 percent of the time?" If that actually occurred, every Sunday would be like Easter, and churches would never lack for financial resources to carry out their ministries. I may be old-fashioned, but it seems to me that our commitment to the church of Jesus Christ our Lord should at least equal our commitment to the Rotary Club!

Of course, being a Christian involves far more than attending weekly worship. It also involves living a life of integrity, being a person of character, having Christian values, being compassionate, serving others, seeking justice, and affirming core beliefs about the life, death, and resurrection of Christ. But sadly, many American Christians exhibit little of this kind of commitment to Jesus Christ.

The Crossed-Out Name of Christ

Some of you have read the novel *Barabbas*. It's a fictional account of what happened to the criminal who was released in the place of Jesus by Pilate, a Roman official in Israel during the time of Christ. In this novel Barabbas became a Roman slave. Rome transported him to Cyprus, where he worked in the copper mines. There he met an old Armenian slave named Sahak, a devout follower of Jesus. Each slave wore a metal disk proclaiming that he belonged to Caesar. But Sahak had strange markings on the back of his disk, which spelled out the name "Christos Jesus." Although he belonged to Caesar, his real allegiance was to Jesus Christ.

Professing that he too wished to follow Jesus, Barabbas asked that his disk be inscribed with the name of Jesus. Working secretly down in the copper mine, they took Barabbas's disk, turned it over, and scratched in the name of Jesus, just like Sahak's disk. But someone overheard them and reported them to the supervisor, who told the governor. Sahak and Barabbas were brought before him. He questioned them about the markings. Sahak said it was the name of his god—Jesus Christ. The governor reminded him that Caesar was their god and warned him that having other gods before Caesar was punishable by death.

The governor questioned Barabbas. "Do you believe in this god Jesus whose name is inscribed on your disk?" Barabbas shook his head. "You don't?" asked the governor. "Why do you bear his name on your disk then?" Barabbas was silent. "Is he your god?" asked the governor. "Isn't that what the inscription means?"

"I have no god," Barabbas answered at last. Sahak gave him a look of despair, pain, and amazement.

Once more Sahak was questioned. "Do you realize the consequences of wearing the name of this god named Jesus?"

"Yes."

"If you renounce your faith in Jesus Christ no harm shall come to you," said the governor. "Will you do it?"

"I cannot," said Sahak. So the governor ordered him to be taken away and crucified.

"Extraordinary man," he said. Then he took a knife and, holding Barabbas's disk in one hand, crossed through the name of Jesus. "There's really no need," the governor said, "as you don't believe in him in any case." And he commended Barabbas for being a sensible fellow and ordered that he be given a better job. And for the rest of his life Barabbas wore the crossed-out name of Jesus on his disk.

That story has haunted me for years. We are not temped to renounce Christ like the early Christians were. On many occasions they were ordered to renounce their faith or die. We know nothing of that kind of religious persecution in America. But the temptation to abandon our faith is still real. Only today it's far more subtle. It happens quietly. We simply drift along, and one day we realize that we have let go of our faith; we realize we have crossed out the name of Christ.

Through the years I've talked to many inactive Christians. I've never met any yet who came to a point where they publicly or privately renounced their faith. They just slowly forgot the importance of God. They quietly fell away. They got busy with other things, even good things like family activities or sporting events or time with friends or career concerns. And they got so busy they forgot to pray or read the Bible or worship God or intentionally serve others. And before they knew it, God, Christ, church, and spiritual issues became unimportant. Slowly but surely they crossed out the name of Christ. More people are lost this way than any other. So be careful. Don't succumb to the temptation to have a halfhearted, casual, nominal Christianity. Don't cross out the name of Christ in your life.

Other Examples of Bad Religion

I could spend a lot of time reviewing other characteristics of bad religion. However, I'm far more interested in exploring good religion, as you will see in part 3. But to further illustrate the point of part 1, other examples of bad religion include the following:

— *anti-intellectual religion* that rejects scientific facts like evolution and climate change;
— *gender-oppressive religion* that tells women they are not equal to men, they must submit to their husbands, and they can't serve as ministers of the gospel;
— *obnoxious religion* that turns people away from God instead of turning them toward God;
— *prosperity religion* that believes in God in order to get material blessings;
— *narcissistic religion* that uses religion as a tool for self-fulfillment rather than a life-style of serving God and others;
— *guilt religion* that tells people they are unworthy and unlovable;
— *exclusive religion* that rejects people who are different from them and that condemns people who disagree with their narrow belief system;
— *legalistic religion* that sees faith as a list of religious rules rather than a relationship with God;
— *bully religion* that intimidates innovative thinkers by labeling them as heretics and enemies of rigid traditions;

— *fatalistic religion* that blames everything that happens in the world on God;
— *privatistic religion* that sees religion solely as personal and neglects the social implications of the gospel;
— *manipulative religion* that preys on people's fears and prejudices;
— *violent religion* that does harm to others in the name of God.

Although additional examples could be given, the main point of part 1 should be clear. Bad religion abounds. So let's now move to the crucial question: What should be our response?

PART 2

IS NOT NO RELIGION

So far we've reviewed several examples of bad religion. These examples raise the question, "What is the proper response to bad religion?" Some argue that the answer to bad religion is no religion. For example, a growing number of "new atheists" argue that since religion can be so toxic, we need to get rid of faith altogether. However, even if we wanted to, we are not going to get rid of religion. Several countries have attempted to terminate religious faith but were unsuccessful. For example, the former Soviet Union tried and failed, along with China. History strongly suggests that you cannot stamp out faith. Somehow people seem to be hardwired to be religious. Human beings seem to be naturally inclined toward religion. The cause of this predisposition toward faith is debated. Some argue it comes from cultural indoctrination. Others say it has its roots in evolutionary adaption. Others affirm it is an essential part of the human spirit created by God.

But regardless of the cause, religion runs deep in human experience. Studies around the world have consistently discovered widespread belief in God, the afterlife, and spiritual realities. For example, a major study at Oxford, called the Cognition, Religion and Theology Project (CRT), strongly implies that religion will not go away. Instead, religion comes naturally, even instinctively, to human begins. Oxford professor Roger Trigg, one of the codirectors of the project, said, "We tend to see purpose in the world. We see agency. We think that something is there even if you can't see it. All of this tends to build up to a religious way of thinking."[1]

On its website, the University of Oxford Institute of Cognitive and Evolutionary Anthropology provides a brief project summary of the CRT. In that summary, the website states, "New empirical research is demonstrating that impulses to religion are part of the most basic ways the human mind works. Religion has always been a feature of human life and is always likely to be. . . . Religious responses to the world, right or wrong, are part of what it is to be human."[2]

Of course, this doesn't prove that God exists. But it does point out how deeply ingrained religion is to human beings and affirms that religion is here to stay for the long haul. Getting rid of it is not going to happen, at least not anytime soon. Even Christopher Hitchens, the late atheist author of *God Is Not Great: How Religion Poisons Everything*, admitted that religion is not going away—"At least not until we get over our fear of death, and of the dark, and of the unknown, and of each other."[3] In spite of the hope of many atheists, riding the world of religion is simply not practical. Far more important, a world with no religion is not helpful and not necessary. To those crucial subjects we now turn our attention.

Notes

1. Richard Allen Greene, "Religious Belief Is Human Nature, Huge New Study Claims," CNN Wire, May 12, 2011, http://religion.blogs.cnn.com/2011/05/12/religious -belief-is-human-nature-huge-new-study-claims/.

2. Justin L. Barrett and Roger Trigg, "Project Summary," University of Oxford, http://www.icea.ox.ac.uk/ labs/projects/cognition-religion-and-theology/project -summary/.

3. Christopher Hitchens, *God Is Not Great: How Religion Poisons Everything* (New York: Hachette, 2007), 12.

6

NO RELIGION
IS NOT HELPFUL

A decade ago Hollywood produced a blockbuster movie called *Troy*, based on the ancient Greek tales of Homer from *The Iliad* and *The Odyssey*. The movie includes a lot of bloody battle scenes and boatloads of computer-generated special effects.

The makers of *Troy* took some liberties with Homer's original story. Some of the changes were minor; some major. But the most radical change was the exclusion of the gods. If you know anything about Homer's classics, you know that the story line was chock-full of the deeds and misdeeds of the Greek gods who resided on Mount Olympus. But in *Troy* the gods were cut. Zeus and Apollo and Athena and all the other deities were completely jettisoned from the story. The filmmakers said they cut the role of the gods to achieve a more realistic film. So instead of Homer's epic story of the gods, *Troy* was reduced to a political tale of human adventure, devoid of religious and spiritual dimensions. Hollywood took Homer's ancient mythological tale of the gods and edited out the gods.

Imagine No Religion

Of course, efforts have been made to get rid of God for a long time. Perhaps the most dramatic effort was made by twentieth-century communism, especially in the Soviet Union and China. Both efforts failed miserably. Today a group called the "new atheists" are trying to rid the world of religion by writing negative books about faith, such as Richard Dawkins's *The God Delusion*, Christopher Hitchens's *God Is Not Great: How Religion Poisons Everything*, and Sam Harris's *Letter to a Christian Nation*. Although the books sold well, atheism has not gained much ground.

Way back in the early 1970s, when I was a teenager, former Beatle John Lennon wrote one of the most popular songs of the twentieth century, "Imagine." In the song Lennon sang, "Imagine there's no heaven," and later added, "And no religion, too." In John Lennon's mind, a world with no religion would be a more enlightened, peaceful, better world. But in my mind and the minds of billions of others, a world without religion would be a sad and gray and terribly impoverished world.

Always Winter but Never Christmas

Many of you have read C. S. Lewis's popular book *The Lion, the Witch, and the Wardrobe*, which tells the story of four children who find their way into a fairy-tale world called Narnia. When they arrive in this magical land, Narnia is in crisis. Narnia is under the spell of the evil White Witch, who keeps Narnia in perpetual winter. In fact, in Narnia, it's always winter but never Christmas. That's what a world would be like without religion: always winter but never Christmas.

Think for a moment about all the good things religion gives us. Religion provides meaning, purpose, and hope for billions of believers. It builds significant relationships and faith communities. It gives people a sense of transcendence. It motivates people to care for others. It promotes responsible ethics and high ideals. It inspires music, art, and beauty. It fosters generosity, law-abidingness, and civic engagement, and even has health benefits. A world without religion would be a bankrupt, impoverished world.

Benefits of Religion

For example, if there were no religion, higher education would look very different. Oxford, Cambridge, Harvard, Yale, and most of the other early colleges were founded by Christian denominations. If religion did not exist, people would be far less educated throughout the world.

If there were no religion, medicine would look different. Early hospitals were built by people of faith who wanted to carry on Christ's healing ministry.

If there were no religion, charity would be greatly diminished. The early church created the first charities. They began by supporting widows and orphans, and that early charitable movement gave birth to virtually every charity we know today, including the Red Cross, the Salvation Army, World Relief, World Vision, Habitat for Humanity, Bread for the World, and many others.

If there were no religion, oppression would be even worse in our world. For example, religion was primarily responsible for ending child labor and slavery. Religion also fueled the civil rights movement in America.

In short, if there were no religion, the world would be a far more dismal place. Even some atheists agree with this assessment—that religion provides society with many benefits. In a *Christian Century* magazine interview with Bruce Sheiman, author of *An Atheist Defends Religion: Why Humanity Is Better Off with Religion Than without It*, Sheiman said, "I don't know if anybody is going to be able to convince me that God exists, but they can convince me that religion has intrinsic value."[1]

As a pastor I see the benefits of religion every day of the week. For example, my previous church sponsors a ministry called Career Transitions that helps hundreds of people a week with the challenges of unemployment. They support an inner-city ministry that makes a huge impact on children and youth in a rough neighborhood. They build a Habitat for Humanity house every year, dramatically changing the life of a family forever. They sponsor a service called Patient Advocacy Ministry that helps people navigate the difficult world of medical insurance. They provide a counseling center that helps thousands of people a year with all kinds of problems from substance abuse to marital discord. They provide music, dance, and art classes for hundreds of people every week. They support medical and other mission work in Honduras, Mexico, and Haiti. They sponsor two schools and a church in South Africa that transform the lives of many children and adults. They provide a large number of support groups for people battling alcoholism or dealing with grief or other human struggles. They are involved in several feeding ministries. They sponsor a winter homeless program called Room in the Inn. They provide a place of significant Christian support and friendship for thousands of people. They lead thousands of people in worship in five different services every weekend, helping them see a God and a world bigger than themselves. And the list goes on and on. Although they are a large congregation, similar ministries occur every day in hundreds of thousands of churches across the country, both large and small, and many thousands more worldwide. So to imagine a world with no religion is to imagine a bleak world indeed, a world where "it's always winter but never Christmas."

Note

1. Bruce Sheiman, interview by Daniel Burke, "Nonbelieving Authors Make Room for Belief," *Christian Century*, November 17, 2009, 14.

7

NO RELIGION
IS NOT NECESSARY

Over the past several months I've been engaged in an ongoing conversation with a young man who calls himself "an agnostic bordering on atheism." When you boil it all down, his primary problems with religion are three-fold:

— the toxic faith of bad religion;
— the belief in a literal Bible;
— the problem of suffering.

I'd like to respond briefly to these three challenges.

Toxic Faith

This young man grew up in a hyperconservative, religious-right, fundamentalist Christian church. By the time he reached his teenage years, he felt completely repulsed by the arrogant, judgmental, closed-minded, antigay, anti-women, antiscience, and highly partisan religion of his parents and his church. As a result he rejected religion altogether. However, as I've already argued, this kind of religion is not authentic faith, is counter to the spirit of Christ, and can and should be rejected. Although some Christians practice this kind of religion, the vast majority of believers do not. So the answer to toxic faith is to leave that faith behind and embrace a more life-giving version of Christianity, which I cover in part 3 of this book.

A Literal Bible

Recently this young man brought his Bible into my office and opened it up to the Old Testament book of Jeremiah. He then proceeded to read several passages from the book. In those passages the people of Israel had been worshiping false gods (idols). In response God, in angry vengeance, killed thousands of Israelites in horribly violent ways. My young friend said, "In these passages God is shown to be a petty, jealous, abusive, murdering, sadistic, terrorist deity. If this is the true nature of God, I don't want to have anything to do with him." Since this young man knows the Bible well, he then complained about other passages in Scripture, including genealogies from Adam to Jesus that, if taken literally, would mean a ten-thousand-year-old earth; a genocidal worldwide flood; the death penalty for working on the Sabbath or being gay; the approval of slavery and polygamy; the subjugation of women by men; and God commanding the genocide of entire communities, including women, children, and even animals. After recounting all of that, he looked at me and said, "How in the world can you believe in a God like that?"

The problem of interpreting the Bible is a complex issue. Since I wrote about this in detail in my previous book, *What's the Least I Can Believe and Still Be a Christian?* I will not cover that same material here. However, I am placing that chapter as an appendix in this book if you would like to dive deeper into the subject. But the bottom line is that believing in a literal Bible is not necessary for Christian believers. In fact, believing in a literal Bible should *not* be affirmed by Christians, for precisely the kinds of reasons my young visitor laid out. A more faithful Christian response is to take the Bible seriously but not always literally. In fact, the Bible never claims to be perfect or "infallible" or "inerrant." It claims only to be inspired.

Although I believe in biblical inspiration and authority, the Bible is also a human document with human limitations, including a prescientific worldview. For example, in the prophet Jeremiah's day, God was understood to be a jealous and wrathful God. However, in the life and teachings of Jesus, we get a better understanding of God, who is far more loving and merciful than Jeremiah understood during his brutal time in history. However, even the "hell-fire and damnation" preacher Jeremiah understood some of those merciful attributes of the Almighty and recorded many of them in his book, which is ultimately a message of hope. In the end, if we are willing to give up a literal interpretation of every passage of Scripture, which is not taught in the Bible and is not the historic faith of the church, many if not most faith problems disappear.

The Problem of Suffering

One of my visits with this young man occurred just days after the horrible mass shooting at an elementary school in Newtown, Connecticut, that killed twenty children and six adults. My young friend talked about this tragic event and asked, "If God exists, why does God allow such terrible things to occur?"

One of the major challenges to religion is the problem of suffering. I don't pretend to have easy and simple answers to this issue. However, Christian believers do have some thoughtful responses to the problem of suffering. I'd like to review them briefly at this time. Because of the complexity of this matter, I'm going to speak in broad strokes. We're going to look at the forest and not the trees.

However, before I begin, I want to remind you of something important: God does not cause suffering. God doesn't get up on Monday morning and say, "I think I'll give a seven-year-old girl a case of leukemia today and send a massive heart attack to a fifty-eight-year-old man and create a twenty-four-car pileup on the highway that kills dozens of people. Oh, and while I'm at it, I think I'll send a huge storm to the northeast United States, kill off sixty more people in Iraq and Afghanistan, and wipe out twenty children along with their teachers at an elementary school in Connecticut." God is not in the business of making people suffer. In the paragraphs that follow, I review ten Christian insights that can help us when we struggle with the problem of suffering.

1. *A limited perspective.* The hard fact is that there are no easy or final answers to the problem of suffering. As Paul says in 1 Corinthians 13, "We see but a poor reflection as in a mirror" (v. 12). We don't have all the answers about suffering, and at least in this life, we never will. So, as we grapple with the problem of suffering, we must admit our ignorance. One day all of this will be made clear, but for now we have a limited perspective.

2. *A world marred by sin.* As Romans 3:23 says, "For all have sinned and fall short of the glory of God." If I were going to put a number to it, I would guess that 90 percent or more of

the world's suffering is caused by sin. God created human beings with free will. Sadly, human beings often abuse that freedom and make terrible choices, which result in suffering. Examples abound. A man, in spite of being warned not to, smokes three packs of cigarettes a day and gets lung cancer and emphysema, causing him and his family great suffering. A young person gets drunk and then drives a car on the highway and kills an entire family, creating awful suffering. And the list could go on and on. Child abuse causes suffering. Crime causes suffering. War causes suffering. Environmental irresponsibility causes suffering. We have poisoned our environment, and now it poisons us. Our environmental sin has gotten so bad it's even changing the weather, causing massive suffering. And in December 2012 a young man either mentally ill or filled with evil went on a shooting spree at an elementary school, causing untold suffering.

The vast majority of suffering in this world is the result of sin. And sin is not just the bad things we do but also the good things we don't do. For example, if we put the time and energy and money into reducing world poverty that we should, suffering in this world would be dramatically reduced. I could go on, but sin causes a huge amount of suffering in the world.

3. *A world that includes evil.* Sometimes human sin, as bad as it can be, doesn't fully explain suffering. There does seem to be a dark power of evil in the world that goes beyond human sinfulness. As Ephesians 6:12 says, "For our struggle is not against flesh and blood, but against . . . the spiritual forces of evil." The Holocaust is perhaps the most vivid example of this kind of evil. That kind of overwhelming evil seems to point to demonic power at work in the world. The Bible doesn't spend a lot of time talking about Satan; there is great mystery here. But in this text and others, the Bible speaks about spiritual forces of evil, which cause suffering in our world.

4. *A life-giving necessity.* In order to have life on our planet, the possibility of suffering is inevitable. Take gravity, for example. We cannot live without gravity. But as you know, gravity sometimes causes suffering. A senior adult falling down and breaking a hip is a good example. Gravity is a life-giving necessity, but it also creates suffering. In order to have life as we know it, some suffering is unavoidable. The laws of nature keep us alive, but sometimes they hurt us. That's the price we have to pay for the gift of life.

Let me give you another, much larger, example. Earthquakes and tsunamis sometimes cause suffering in our world. They are caused by shifts in the crust of the earth. Our planet could not support life without some shifting in the crust of the earth. So the earth's crust, which allows us to live on this planet, sometimes results in suffering. Like gravity, the shifting crust of the earth is a life-giving necessity. But it also causes suffering. In short, you cannot have life on our planet without pain. Suffering is the price we pay for the gift of being alive.

5. *A God who suffers.* The cross of Jesus Christ does not explain suffering. But it does tell us that God is not an aloof God, cut off from human struggle. Instead, God is a God of the cross, a crucified God, who fully enters human pain and suffering. So when the world suffers, or when we personally suffer, we are never alone. God suffers with us. The older I get and the more suffering I see, the more important this becomes to me.

6. *A God who comforts.* Not only does God suffer with those who suffer, but God also provides comfort. That comfort comes in many different forms. God comforts us directly, through the Holy Spirit, giving us strength and courage to face suffering. God also comforts us indirectly, primarily through other people who love and support and help us through times of suffering. When people suffer, God is in the business of offering comfort.

7. *A church that serves.* Part of God's answer to the problem of suffering is the church's response to suffering. For example, I once went to visit a member of our congregation who was in critical care at the hospital. When I arrived, several members of our church were already there, giving love and support to that suffering family. Still others gave support by mowing their grass, providing food, and offering other tangible services. When people suffer, the church responds. And this doesn't just happen on an individual basis. It's much bigger than that. Worldwide service organizations like Habitat for Humanity, Bread for the World, Compassion International, the Red Cross, Presbyterian Disaster Assistance, and the United Methodist Committee on Relief are all examples of God alleviating suffering through the service of others, especially the service of the church. Whenever suffering occurs in this world, the church is always there, reducing suffering in the name of Christ.

8. *An opportunity to grow.* I wish it were not so, but most human growth comes through suffering. Hard times, more than anything else, build character and perseverance. That's been true in my life. The times I've grown the most are the times I've struggled the most. I'm not saying that God makes us suffer in order for us to grow. But God uses the suffering that comes our way to help make us better people. Of course, we need to be careful here. We don't need to go to someone who just lost a loved one, lost a job, or received a diagnosis of cancer and say, "This is a great opportunity for you to grow." That would be callous and uncaring. But the fact is that suffering often results in significant growth.

As we read in James 1:2–4 (TNIV), "Consider it pure joy, my brothers and sisters, whenever you face trials of many kinds, because you know that the testing of your faith develops perseverance. Let perseverance finish its work so that you may be mature and complete." For example, I've talked with numerous cancer survivors who told me that while it was awful to get and fight and beat cancer, it was also the best thing that ever happened to them. One person told me that her cancer brought her to God, clarified her values, connected her to others, and made her a dramatically better person. I'm not suggesting God brings suffering on us in order to make us better people. Nor should we elevate suffering to the level of a spiritual discipline. But God, in God's mercy, does use the hard times that come our way to help us grow.

9. *A world full of good*. Sometimes, when we watch the evening news, it's easy to think the whole world is in misery. But that's just not true. In spite of some very real suffering, the world is full of life and joy and love and good. For example, over the past week, several people in your community were victims of crime, several were rushed to the hospital, and a few died. But during that same time thousands of people in your community went to work every day, loved their family, ate lunch with their friends, did community service, played soccer after school, went to church on Sunday, and tucked in their children at night with a kiss—and not just in your community but all over the world.

Yes, twenty-six people were killed at a mass school shooting in Newtown, Connecticut, in December 2012 by a deeply disturbed person. But on that same day millions of other children went to school, learned new things, enjoyed their friends, and were not hurt. Don't forget that! Most people in the world are *not* suffering today. So, in the midst of pain, let us remember that wonderful things are happening all over the world—things that don't make the evening news. As Paul reminds us in Philippians 4:8 (TNIV), "Whatever is true, whatever is noble, whatever is right, whatever is pure, whatever is lovely, whatever is admirable—if anything is excellent or praiseworthy— think about such things."

10. *A future of hope.* Finally, we need to remember that one day all suffering will come to an end. In the final kingdom of God, there will be no more pain, no more tears, no more cancer, no more war, no more crime, no more hurricanes, and no more school shootings. As John affirms in Revelation 21, "Then I saw 'a new heaven and a new earth.' . . . 'He will wipe every tear from their eyes. There will be no more death' or mourning or crying or pain" (vv. 1, 4).

I realize that these ten Christian insights don't answer all our questions about suffering. As I said in the beginning, we have a limited perspective; we see through the glass darkly. But these insights are enough to keep us going until the day finally arrives when God outlaws suffering forever and makes all things new.

An Agnostic Bordering on Faith

After visiting with my young friend many times over the course of several months, we covered in detail his three major problems with Christianity. We discussed that toxic religion, including judgmental, negative, absolutist, and closed-minded faith, is not normative Christianity and can and should be rejected. We agreed that biblical literalism is not a necessary, historic, or even biblical belief; that it causes enormous and unnecessary theological problems; and that it can and should be jettisoned. Finally, we agreed that while final and easy answers to the problem of suffering are not available, helpful and thoughtful Christian insights and responses to this challenge do exist.

The last time I spoke to this young man, he told me he was no longer "an agnostic bordering on atheism" but "an agnostic bordering on faith." I saw him at church a few weeks ago at one of our worship services. During Communion he came forward to receive the elements. When I handed him the bread and said, "This is the body of Christ given for you," he smiled at me. I hope to see him again soon.

PART 3

BUT GOOD RELIGION

On July 28, 2010, ex–Roman Catholic novelist Anne Rice posted her "resignation" as a Christian on her Facebook account. She said, "Today I quit being a Christian. I'm out." She said she was still committed to Jesus Christ, but she was rejecting Christianity. In her post she added, "I refuse to be anti-feminist. I refuse to be anti-artificial birth control. I refuse to be anti-Democrat. I refuse to be anti-science. I refuse to be anti-life. In the name of Christ, I quit Christianity and being Christian."

Soon after Anne Rice posted this on Facebook, her message went viral. I read about it online and soon thereafter saw the story in my local newspaper. As I read her Facebook posting, I had two strong emotional responses. First, I resonated with her words. Like Anne Rice, I reject intolerant, ignorant, closed-minded, judgmental, negative, bad religion. I understood exactly what she was saying and why she was saying it. On the other hand, I found myself wanting to shout at the top of my lungs, "There is another option!" Just because some people practice bad religion doesn't mean we have to ditch religion altogether. The answer to bad religion is not *no religion*. Instead, the answer to bad religion is *good religion*.

Jesus understood that. In the face of the arrogant, judgmental, and legalistic religion of his day, Jesus offered a healthy alternative of humility, grace, mercy, compassion, and justice. Promoting that kind of religion is what moderate and mainline churches are all about, including my own denomination, the United Methodist Church. Moderate and mainline churches are not perfect by any stretch. But we try to offer healthy faith to the world. We promote a religion of grace, not judgment; a religion of love, not hatred; a religion of open-mindedness, not intolerance; a religion of compassion, not legalism; and a religion of humility, not arrogance.

We'll now review some characteristics of "good" religion. As in part 1, these examples are certainly not comprehensive. However, they do offer examples of good religion. Since my last book focused on healthy religious beliefs, the following chapters focus on healthy religious practices.

8

⁓

GOOD RELIGION
IMPACTS THE WAY WE LIVE

As a man drove down a busy street, an impatient and stressed-out woman closely tailgated him. Suddenly the light turned yellow just in front of him. He did the right thing and stopped at the crosswalk, even though he could have beaten the red light by accelerating through the intersection. The tailgating woman went ballistic, honked her horn over and over, and screamed in frustration as she missed her chance to get through the intersection. As she continued her ranting, she heard a tap on her window and looked up into the face of a serious-looking police officer. The officer ordered her to exit her car with her hands up. He took her to the police station where she was searched, fingerprinted, photographed, and placed in a holding cell.

After a couple of hours, another policeman released her. He escorted her back to the booking desk where the arresting officer waited with her personal effects. He said, "I'm very sorry for this mistake. You see, when I pulled up behind your car, you were blowing your horn, making obscene gestures to the guy in front of you, and cursing a blue streak at him. I noticed the "What Would Jesus Do?" bumper sticker, the "Choose Life" license plate holder, the "Follow Me to Sunday School" bumper sticker, and the chrome-plated Christian fish emblem on the trunk. Naturally, I assumed you had stolen the car."

I laughed when I heard that story, but it communicates a painful truth. A lot of us who claim to be Christians don't always live like Christians.

"If All My Religion Is Going to Change Is My Sunday Schedule, Then I'm Not Interested"

I'm not saying Christians should be perfect people. We'll never attain perfection. But our faith does need to impact our lives — every part of our lives. I recently heard about a young man who said, "If all my religion is going to change is my Sunday schedule, then I'm not interested. I want something that is going to change my finances, my sex life, the way I work, the way I treat my family, the way I treat others, and the way I use my time."

This young man understands something important. Authentic faith needs to impact every part of our lives. For example, our religion should have a significant impact on how we spend our money. The fact that the average American Christian gives less than 2 percent of his or her income to charity is a serious problem. If we took our faith seriously, we'd spend far less on ourselves and far more on charitable work. Our faith should also have a huge impact on how we work; how we treat our family, friends, neighbors, and coworkers; and how we use our time. Our faith should impact how we treat the environment and how we treat the poor. Our faith should impact our character, ethics, and values. In short, our faith as Christians should make a huge impact on every aspect of our lives.

We see this theme throughout the Bible. For example, in the Old Testament, Joshua says to the people of Israel, "Choose for yourselves this day whom you will serve" (Josh. 24:15). He then told them to take their commitment to God seriously. The Bible provides hundreds of other examples. For example, in the book of Romans, Paul says that our faith should impact virtually every aspect of our life. In chapter 12 Paul writes,

> Love must be sincere. Hate what is evil; cling to what is good. Be devoted to one another in brotherly love. Honor one another above yourselves. Never be lacking in zeal, but keep your spiritual fervor, serving the Lord. Be joyful in hope, patient in affliction, faithful in prayer. Share with the Lord's people who are in need. Practice hospitality.
> (Rom. 12:9–13)

Paul continues this theme not only in Romans but in all of his writings in the New Testament. In short, the Bible teaches that good religion impacts our lives in tangible and practical ways.

God Is More Important Than Sports

Several months ago I heard a story about a seventh-grade girl in Texas. She ran on the junior high girls' track team at her school. Due to bad weather an important Saturday track meet got postponed to the next Saturday. However, this girl had already committed to be on a church mission trip on that Saturday. She went to her track coach and told him about the conflict. He told her, "Your teammates are counting on you, and you can't let them down. I expect you to be here for the meet." She went home in tears. The next day she talked to the coach again. He responded, "You are either here for the meet or you turn in your uniform." More tears from her that night. The next day she went to her coach for a third time, handed him her uniform, and walked away. That evening she explained her decision to her family. She said, "This is about God. And God is more important than sports."

Since the rest of part 3 deals with this overall theme of taking faith seriously, I'll end with the following story.

Under the Cross of Christ

A few years ago I heard about a teacher who, while cleaning out her attic, came upon a cross she purchased years earlier. It was a crucifix—a wooden cross with a silver image of Jesus hanging on it. She put the cross on her home office desk and left it there for several days. However, she needed some space to work, so she laid the cross on top of her checkbook and her bills. Underneath the small body of Jesus, she could see how many frequent flyer miles she had earned that month for charging expenses to her American Express card. It made her think about how her faith should impact her finances. If her money were really under the cross of Jesus, what would she buy? What would she not buy? How much would she give away? How much would she keep? It was a strange thing, looking at the crucified Christ lying on top of her checkbook.

A few days later she put the crucifix on top of some papers she was grading for her students. It made her think about how her faith should impact her work. If her job were really under the cross of Jesus, how would she treat her students? Her colleagues? How would she prepare for her classes?

A few days later she put the cross on top of some recent photographs of her family and friends. It made her think about how her faith should impact her relationships. If her relationships were really under the cross of Jesus, what kind of wife would she be, what kind of mother, what kind of grandmother, what kind of friend? For several weeks that cross lay on her desk, and it seemed to ask her, on a daily basis, "What difference does my faith make in my life? What impact does my religion have on my finances, my job, and my relationships?" These questions are good and important to ask, because good religion profoundly impacts the way we live.

9

GOOD RELIGION
PRIORITIZES LOVE

Several years ago Hollywood released a movie called *Up in the Air*. In one scene a young man is about to get married. It's just a few minutes before the ceremony begins, but he has cold feet. He's not sure he can go through with the wedding. So a member of the family, played by George Clooney, goes to talk to him. The young man says, "I don't think I'll be able to do this."

Clooney's character asks, "Why would you say that today?"

The frightened young man says,

Well, last night I was kinda like laying in bed, and I couldn't get to sleep, so I started thinking about the wedding and the ceremony and about our buying a house, and moving in together, and having a kid, and then having another kid, and then Christmas and Thanksgiving and spring break, and going to football games, and then all of a sudden they are graduated and getting jobs and getting married and, you know, I'm a grandparent, and then I'm retired, and I'm losing my hair, and I'm getting fat, and the next thing I know I'm dead. And it's like, I can't stop from thinking, "What's the point?" I mean, what is the point?

What's the Point?

No question is more important than that one: What is the point? People answer that question differently. For some people finances are the point. They work hard to accumulate financial assets. They put money into stocks and bonds and real estate and IRAs and 401(k)s. The problem is that finances are not dependable. A crash in the market, a layoff, a business failure, a disability, the death of a spouse, a recession—any of these can wipe out our financial security. If finances are the primary point of life, we could be in real trouble.

Some people make their job the primary point of their life. They invest enormous hours into their career, trying to climb to the top. They work hard to earn job security. The problem is that job security is a myth. In this day of outsourcing and corporate downsizing, we can lose our jobs literally overnight. If our job is the main point of our life, we could be in real trouble.

For other people physical health is the point. They walk and jog and go to the gym and eat healthy food and watch their cholesterol. The problem is that our health is not dependable. It can go south at any time and at any age. If health is the primary point for us, we could be in real trouble.

For many people family is the main point. We depend much on our family, as we should. The problem is that loved ones are not always dependable. They grow up, they move away, they die, and sometimes they leave or say they want a divorce. As important as family is, if that's the main point of our life, we could be in real trouble.

Finances, work, health, and family—all are important. But if any of these are the primary point of our life, we could be in real trouble. Why? Because these things are not dependable. None are completely secure. All are tentative, temporary, and easily lost.

So, what is the point? More specifically, what is the point of religion, especially Christian religion? According to the Bible, the point is love. When Jesus was asked, "Of all the commandments, which is the most important?" he responded, "Love the Lord your God with all your heart and with all your soul and with all your mind and with all your strength" (Mark 12:30). The apostle Paul, in 1 Corinthians 13 said, "And now these three remain: faith, hope and love. But the greatest of these is love" (v. 13). John said, "Dear friends, let us love one another, for love comes from God. Everyone who loves has been born of God and knows God. Whoever does not love does not know God, because God is love" (1 John 4:7–8).

Do You Love Me?

According to Jesus, Paul, John, and the entire Bible, the point is love. However, love in the Bible is not some kind of warm, fuzzy feeling. Love is concrete and shows itself in action. For example, in what people often call the "love chapter" of the Bible, Scripture says, "Love is patient, love is kind. It does not envy, it does not boast, it is not proud. It does not dishonor others, it is not self-seeking, it is not easily angered, it keeps no record of wrongs. Love does not delight in evil but rejoices with the truth. It always protects, always trusts, always hopes, always perseveres. Love never fails" (1 Cor. 13:4–8a TNIV). All these characteristics of love listed in 1 Corinthians 13 are action-based, not emotion-based.

Many of you have seen the classic musical *Fiddler on the Roof*. In one scene the main characters, Tevye and Golde, discuss love. They lived in a culture and day when marriages were arranged by parents. They didn't even meet until their wedding day. However, the times were changing. Their daughters wanted to marry for love. So in this scene Tevye asks his wife, "Do you love me?" At first she resists his question, but he presses her to answer. Finally she replies that over the past twenty-five years she has washed his clothes, cooked his meals, cleaned his house, and even milked his cow. Later she adds, "For twenty-five years I've lived with him, fought with him, starved with him, twenty-five years my bed is his. If that's not love, what is?" As Golde understood, real love is love that shows itself in action, love that makes a difference in the way we live. With that as a backdrop, let's talk a bit more about the Great Commandment of Christ, which is about loving God, loving neighbor, and loving self.

The Great Commandment

Loving God. The Great Commandment begins by saying, "Love the Lord your God with all your heart and with all your soul and with all your mind and with all your strength" (Mark 12:30). The first point of the Great Commandment is to love God. As we've already mentioned, this doesn't just refer to emotional love, although that element of faith is certainly appropriate. During worship or prayer, people often have feelings of emotive love for God. Last winter, when my wife and I went on vacation, I took a late afternoon walk on the beach as the sun was setting. I was all alone on the beach, the sunset was amazing, and I felt deeply moved by the beauty of God's creation. I spontaneously begin to sing "How Great Thou Art" and followed it by singing a contemporary praise song. It was a moment of awe and praise and strong emotional love for God. But to love God with all our being is far more than feelings of emotional love. It means, at the very least, that we practice historic spiritual disciplines including worship, prayer, Bible readings, and generous financial offerings to God's work. As one bumper sticker says, "If you love Jesus, tithe. Anyone can honk!"

Several years ago I heard a story that has bothered me ever since. The story is about a young disciple in India who left his home in search of a well-known spiritual master. He finally found the great teacher sitting in prayer beside a river. The young man begged the master to teach him. The master rose slowly, then suddenly grabbed the young man and dragged him into the river and plunged his head under the water. Seconds passed, then about half a minute, then a full minute. The young man struggled and kicked, but still the teacher held his head under the water. Finally, he pulled the young man, who was coughing and gasping, out of the water. After the young man caught his breath, the teacher asked him, "While you were under the water, what did you want?"

"Air," the young man replied, still panting.

The master asked, "And how badly did you want it?"

The young man said, "It was all I wanted in the world. With my whole soul I longed only for air."

"Good," said the teacher. "When you long for God in the same way you have just now longed for air, come back to me and you will become my disciple."

The reason that story has bothered me so much is that I'm not sure I want God as badly as that young man wanted air. I'm not sure I love God that much. But I *want* to love God that much. And *wanting* to love God that much is a good beginning.

Loving neighbor. The second part of the Great Commandment is to love others. After saying that the greatest commandment is to love God with all our heart, mind, soul, and strength, Jesus added, "Love your neighbor as yourself" (Mark 12:31 NRSV). Throughout the Bible we see that the best way to express our love for God is to love other people.

In Luke's Gospel, there's a famous story called the parable of the Good Samaritan. In this story a lawyer asks Jesus what he must do to inherit eternal life. Jesus asks him, "What is written in the Law?" The lawyer responds that we should love God and neighbor. Jesus affirms the man by saying, "You have answered correctly. . . . Do this and you will live." But the lawyer is not fully satisfied with the answer. So he asks Jesus, "And who is my neighbor?" (Luke 10:25–29).

In response to the question, Jesus tells the familiar story of the Good Samaritan. In Jesus' day, Samaritans were considered half-breeds, and most Jews despised them. In this story a Samaritan helps a Jewish man who is robbed and beaten up on a business trip. You may recall that two other, very religious people, including a priest, walk right past the beaten man without helping. Only the Samaritan stops to provide assistance. Jesus ends the story by asking the lawyer, "Which of these three do you think was a neighbor to the man who fell into the hands of the robbers?" The lawyer says, "The one who had mercy on him." Jesus replies, "Go and do likewise" (Luke 10:36–37).

The point of the parable is that we are called to love others, especially people who are different from us. That's not always easy, but it's the call of Christ on our lives. A few years ago I heard a powerful story that illustrates what it means to love our neighbor, especially neighbors who are different from us.

The story comes from the Heartsong Church, a United Methodist congregation in Cordova, Tennessee, a suburb of Memphis. A few years ago the Heartsong Church found out that a mosque was going to be built right next to its property. At first the church felt startled. Some of the members were angry, many were fearful, and almost all of them were uncomfortable. But as they discussed the situation, they asked themselves the question, "What would Jesus do?" In spite of their fears and prejudices, the question, "What would Jesus do?" was easy to answer. Jesus would love his neighbors, as he taught in the Great Commandment. In fact, Jesus even teaches us to love our enemies. So they put up a big sign in front of the church that said, "Heartsong Church Welcomes Memphis Islamic Center to the Neighborhood." But that's not the end of the story.

When the church found out that the mosque construction was not going to be completed in time for the Muslim holy month of Ramadan, Heartsong invited the Muslim group to use its sanctuary for worship and prayer. That amazed me. It's one thing to let the Presbyterians use your church, maybe even the Pentecostals. But the Muslims? And they didn't just let them use the space. They posted greeters at the church to welcome their Muslim neighbors as they walked into the church. I saw this story on the evening news. In the news story a reporter interviewed some of the members of the church. One woman said, "I've never met a Muslim in my life. But I've made friends with one of the women from the mosque and found out we have a lot in common." Several others had similar comments. The Islamic community now refers to the Heartsong Church as their "Christian brothers and sisters." When the reporter asked the pastor of the church why his congregation responded in this way, the pastor said, "Because Jesus teaches us to love our neighbors."

Loving self. In the Great Commandment Jesus tells us to love God, and then he tells us to love our neighbor "as ourselves." So the final section of the Great Commandment is the command to love ourselves. I'm certainly not talking about a self-absorbed, narcissistic kind of self-love. That's counter to everything Jesus taught and did. But it's important that we affirm and internally accept that we are beloved children of God with value and dignity and worth. To help illustrate that point I want to share one of my favorite stories.

I See the Family Resemblance

Many years ago, on a trip through Tennessee, a retired minister and seminary professor named Fred Craddock stopped into a restaurant where he met an old man, long retired. When the elderly gentlemen found out that Craddock was a preacher, he told him the following story from his childhood.

The old man told Craddock that he had been born and raised in a little village near that restaurant. He had a single mother, and they were very poor. He was what they called back then an "illegitimate child," a child born out of wedlock. When his mother and he came into town on Saturday, they were shunned by all the good people. They wouldn't let their kids play with him, and some of them walked on the other side of the street when they saw his mother and him coming. He had many fights with boys at school over the names they called him and the bad things they said about his mother.

They had a little church in that village. The boy went to it sometimes. He would sneak in after the service started and slip out before the benediction so that he would not have to face the church people and feel their disapproval. One day a new pastor came to the church. To check him out, the boy slipped into a back pew halfway through the service. And he liked the sermon. The pastor was young and talked so that the boy could understand him.

But then the new preacher pulled a fast one on the boy. After the sermon he walked to the back of the church, announced that he wanted to meet everyone present, and then pronounced the benediction. The boy was trapped. He waited until the church was empty, hunkered down in the corner, hoping the pastor would not notice him. But he did. The new preacher walked over to him, thrust out his hand, and said, "Glad to see you, boy. And tell me, who is your daddy?"

The boy turned red and dropped his head. The preacher didn't know the details, but he knew he had asked the wrong question. The pastor took the boy by the chin, pulled his face up to look him straight in the eye, and said, "Oh, you don't need to tell me. I already know. I see the family resemblance. I see it in your face. You are a child of God."

The boy's name was Ben Hooper. He went on to become the governor of the state of Tennessee. Imagine that! Through that and other experiences, Ben Hooper learned that he was a beloved child of God with worth, value, and dignity. Affirming that truth is one part of living out the Great Commandment.

An entire book could be written on the Great Commandment to love God and to love our neighbor as ourselves. In the end that's what matters most. Jesus knew that love is the most powerful force in the world—more powerful that military, economic, or political power and more powerful than hatred, fear, prejudice, and violence. So good religion prioritizes love. That's the point.

10

GOOD RELIGION
ENGAGES IN SERVICE

Since this emphasis on service is so similar to the previous one on prioritizing love, I'll keep it short and simple. But the topic of service to others is too important not to develop further. As a part of living out the Great Commandment to love our neighbor, good religion constantly encourages believers to engage in service to other people for at least three reasons. First, we engage in service for God's sake. When we give our time, energy, and resources in the service of humanity, we follow the example of Christ and bring joy to God. Second, we engage in service for others' sake. Huge numbers of people in the world, locally and beyond, are hurting—physically, emotionally, and spiritually—and they need assistance. Third, we engage in service for our own sake. The only way to find true meaning and fulfillment in life is to get beyond ourselves and engage in service with people in need. As Proverbs 11:25 says, "A generous person will be enriched, and one who gives water will get water" (NRSV).

In Matthew 25, Jesus tells a story about the last judgment. In that story he doesn't say we'll be judged on our faith or theology. Instead, Jesus says we'll be judged based on how we treated people in need. In this passage Jesus said,

> Then the king will say to those at his right hand, "Come, you that are blessed by my Father, inherit the kingdom prepared for you from the foundations of the world; for I was hungry and you gave me food, I was thirsty and you gave me something to drink, I was a stranger and you welcomed me, I was naked and you gave me clothing, I was sick and you took care of me, I was in prison and you visited me." Then the righteous will answer him, "Lord, when was it that we saw you hungry and gave you food, or thirsty and gave you something to drink? And when was it that we saw you a stranger and welcomed you, or naked and gave you clothing? And when was it that we saw you sick or in prison and visited you?" And the king will answer them, "Truly I tell you, just as you did it to one of the least of these who are members of my family, you did it to me."
>
> (Matt. 25:34–40, NRSV)

There is no ambiguity in this passage. Jesus is clear. The best way to serve God is to serve others. When we do, we are serving Jesus himself. I'll illustrate that truth by telling you one of my all-time favorite stories.

The Bread and the Ark

At the beginning of the sixteenth century, the Jews were expelled from Spain. Many went to France, Germany, and Greece; some went to the Holy Land. Among them was Jacoby, a shoemaker by trade. Jacoby was a kind man, but most of all, Jacoby was a devout man. He went to the synagogue every Sabbath and listened to what the rabbi was saying, even though Jacoby spoke Spanish and the rabbi spoke Hebrew.

One Sabbath the rabbi mentioned in his sermon how at one time loaves of bread were offered to God. Jacoby heard and understood the words *bread* and *God*, and he got excited. He ran home and said to his wife, "Esperanza! Guess what? God eats bread! And you are the best baker in the whole country! This week make your best bread, and I'll bring it to God." That week Esperanza kneaded in the best ingredients and braided the dough with such love. Jacoby then took the seven loaves of bread to the synagogue. "Señior Dios," Jacoby said to God. "I've got your bread. You will love it. My wife, Esperanza, she's a wonderful baker! You'll eat every crumb!" Then Jacoby took the bread and put it into the holy ark.

No sooner did Jacoby leave than in came the shammes, the man who cleans up the synagogue. "Lord, you know I want to be here in this holy place; that's all I want to do. But for seven weeks now I haven't been paid. Lord, I need for you to make me a miracle. I believe you're going to; maybe you have done it already. Maybe I'll open the holy ark, and there will be my miracle." He walked to the ark and opened it, and there was his miracle. Seven loaves of bread! Enough for the whole week. The next day, when the rabbi opened up the ark and Jacoby and Esperanza saw that the bread was gone, you should have seen the look of love that passed between them. The next week it was the same. And the week after. This went on for months. The shammes learned to have faith in God, but he also realized that if he came to the synagogue too early, there was no miracle. And so thirty years went by.

Now an old man, Jacoby came one day to the syna-gogue with his loaves of bread. "Señior Dios," he prayed,

"I know your bread's been lumpy lately. Esperanza's arthritis—maybe you could do something? You'll eat better!"

He put the bread in the ark and started to leave when suddenly the rabbi grabbed him. "What are you doing?" the rabbi demanded.

"I'm bringing God his bread," Jacoby replied.

"God doesn't eat bread!" said the rabbi.

Jacoby said, "He's been eating Esperanza's bread for thirty years."

At that moment the two men heard a noise, and they hid.

No sooner did they hide than in came the shammes. "I hate to bring it up, Lord, but you know your bread's been lumpy lately. Maybe you could talk to an angel." When the shammes reached into the ark for the loaves of bread, the rabbi jumped out and grabbed him. The rabbi angrily told the two men that what they were doing was sinful, going on and on, and soon all three men began to cry. Jacoby cried because he only wanted to do good. The rabbi cried because his sermon thirty years ago had caused this. And the shammes cried because there would be no more bread.

Suddenly they heard laughter from the corner. They turned and saw the great mystic Rabbi Isaac. Shaking his head and laughing, Rabbi Isaac said, "No, Rabbi, these men, they are not sinful. These men are devout! You should know that God has never had more pleasure than watching what goes on in your synagogue. On the Sabbath, he sits with his angels, and they laugh, watching this man bring the bread and the other man take the bread, while God gets all the credit! You must beg forgiveness of these men, Rabbi."

Rabbi Isaac looked at Jacoby and said, "Jacoby, you must do something even more difficult. You must now bring your bread directly to the shammes, and when you do, you must believe with perfect faith that it is the same as giving it to God."

"You must now bring your bread directly to the shammes, and when you do, you must believe with perfect faith that it is the same as giving it to God." That sounds a lot like another rabbi named Jesus, a man who said, "To the extent that you did it unto the least of these, you did it unto me."

11

GOOD RELIGION PROVIDES A PROPHETIC VOICE

Years ago an oppressive political system called apartheid ruled in South Africa. In that system a small minority of whites totally oppressed the black majority. But in that darkness, people began to imagine a different future. People like Nelson Mandela and Desmond Tutu began to dream of a democratic and free South Africa. They began to take steps toward that dream, which landed them in a lot of trouble.

One day Archbishop Tutu was preaching a sermon at an ecumenical service at the Cathedral of Saint George in South Africa. In the sermon he shared his dream of a free South Africa. At that moment members of the notorious South African Security Police broke into the cathedral. They brought guns and tape recorders and cameras in an effort to threaten and cower Tutu and everyone there. Just a few weeks earlier they had arrested the archbishop and put him in jail for several days. But this man of God had a vision for a free South Africa, and he was not about to be intimidated.

He stared at the police for a while, and he even acknowledged their power. He said, "You men are powerful, very powerful." But he then reminded them that he served a higher power than their political authority. He said, "I serve a God who cannot be mocked!" Then, in an extraordinary challenge to politically tyranny, Archbishop Desmond Tutu told these representatives of South African apartheid, "Since you have already lost, I invite you today to come and join the winning side!" He said it with a smile on his face but with a clarity and boldness that took everyone's breath away.

The congregation's response was electric. The crowd was literally transformed by the archbishop's challenge to power. In spite of hundreds of well-armed security police surrounding them, the congregation literally leaped to their feet and shouted praises to God, and then they began to dance!

These people dared to imagine a different future, a future free from oppression, a future of freedom and democracy; that vision gave them the strength to stand up against the forces of oppression. Not many years later the corrupt system of apartheid collapsed, and South Africa became a democracy. But it all began with a handful of religious people who dared to imagine a different future.[1]

Times exist when religion must challenge the culture. It must do so lovingly and humbly but also clearly and boldly. One of the characteristics of good religion is providing a prophetic voice when that voice is needed. In today's American culture the church needs to challenge numerous conditions. Two examples follow.

Challenging Consumerism

In spite of Jesus' warning that a person cannot love God and money at the same time and his command not to store up treasure on earth, we are a highly consumerist culture.

It's hard not to be. We are bombarded daily with messages to buy more and more stuff. In fact, buying more stuff than we can afford and putting it on credit, from credit cards to mortgages, was one of the major causes of the Great Recession that began in 2008. It's easy in America to get sucked into the trap of accumulation, which reminds me of the following old Indian parable.

A guru had a star disciple. He was so pleased with the man's spiritual progress that he left him on his own. The disciple lived in a little mud hut. His only clothing was a loincloth, a small covering around his midsection. He lived simply, begging for his food. Each morning after his devotions, the disciple washed his loincloth and hung it out to dry. One day he came back to discover the loincloth torn and eaten by rats. He begged the villagers for another loincloth, and they gave it to him. But the rats ate that one, too. So he got himself a cat.

That took care of the rats, but now when he begged for his food, he had to beg for milk for his cat. *This won't do*, he thought, *I'll get a cow*. So he got a cow to feed his cat, but now he had to beg for hay to feed his cow. So in order to feed his cow, he decided to till and plant the ground around his hut. But soon he found no time for contemplation, so he hired servants to tend his farm.

Overseeing the laborers became a chore, so he got married to have a wife to help him with the farm. His wife didn't like the mud hut he lived in and demanded a real and large home. She also wanted nice furniture and lots of clothes. So the man had to grow even more crops and hire more servants to keep his wife happy. In time the disciple became the wealthiest man in the village.

Years later this man's guru was traveling nearby, so he stopped in to see his old student. He was shocked by what he saw. Where once stood a simple mud hut now loomed a palace surrounded by a vast estate, worked by many servants. "What is the meaning of this?" he asked his disciple.

"You won't believe this, sir," the disciple replied. "But there was no other way I could keep my loincloth."

In America it's easy to get sucked into a materialistic lifestyle of accumulation. But in the end, material consumption does not lead to a better life. For example, every year in this country, a major survey measures the level of contentment and happiness among Americans. These happiness surveys go all the way back to the 1950s. In case you weren't around — or have forgotten — let me remind you of life in the fifties. In the 1950s most Americans lived in small houses. Most families owned only one car that might have had an AM radio. But it did not have a CD player or cruise control, navigation system, air-conditioning, or much of anything else we expect today. TVs, if you were lucky enough to own one, were in black-and-white, and there were only three channels. People didn't have air-conditioning, computers, the Internet, cable TV, or smart phones. I could go on, but you get the picture.

Contrast all of that with life today. Life in America in the twenty-first century has dramatically improved since 1950. The average family income, even after being adjusted for inflation, is double what it was in 1950. The square footage of the average American home has doubled. Most families own at least two cars loaded with options nobody could have dreamed of in 1950. TVs today are not only in color, but they also come in big screen and high definition and 3-D, with hundreds of channels to choose from. Almost everyone has a personal computer or a tablet. Virtually everyone today owns a cell phone or smart phone. Our homes, our offices, and even our cars are air-conditioned.

But in spite of all these increases in material possessions and our standard of living, the percentage of Americans who describe themselves as happy and content has not budged since the 1950s. We are not one iota happier than we were fifty years ago, in spite of dramatic improvements in our standard of living. In fact, our happiness levels have decreased. We've conducted a sixty-year-plus experiment to see if a higher standard of living makes people content and happy and learned that it does not. The promise that consumption will bring us happiness is an American myth, a lie. Acquiring more stuff does not lead to contentment, and more important, it is an enemy to the spiritual life, distracting us from what matters most. Oveconsumption also does great damage to God's planet. And it keeps us from being generous to God's work and those in need. Therefore, good religion must challenge the American obsession with accumulating more and more stuff.

Challenging Environmental Irresponsibility

During my seminary years my family and I lived in student housing—a large apartment complex owned by the seminary called Seminary Village. Seminarians affectionately referred to Seminary Village as the "Gospel Ghetto." Most everyone who lived at the Gospel Ghetto was broke, so the seminary provided us a large field for planting gardens. They figured if we could grow our own food, at least we wouldn't starve! Our garden plot was plot number 26. In the spring we planted our garden. We spent many hours tilling, planting, and caring for garden plot number 26. From the start we saw that it was a fine work. The tomato plants grew rapidly, the flowers bloomed, and the beans pushed their stalks toward the sky. We were proud of our garden and waited in anticipation for the coming fruits of our labor.

One afternoon, however, I received a phone call from a concerned neighbor. She said, "Are you the owners of garden plot number 26?"

"Yes," I replied.

"I hate to tell you," she said, "but some children have messed up your garden. You better come look."

We immediately went to the garden. It had been ravaged. The tomato plants had been pulled up by their roots, the stakes knocked down, the flowers uprooted, and the beans trampled upon. My wife and I were left with a seriously vandalized garden. We had to make a decision. Fall was coming. Was it too late in the season to start over?

Our garden story serves as a parable of what humanity has done to our planet. Like vandalistic children we have ravaged garden Earth. Toxic waste, air pollution, deforestation, topsoil erosion, polluted water, oil spills, acid rain, solid-waste disposal, and climate change are just a few of the massive environmental problems we face today. Fall is coming. We must act now if we want to save planet Earth.

The Christian community must speak out on behalf of God's creation. Earth care is a deeply spiritual practice. For far too long the church has remained silent on this subject. Sadly many churches in America resist environmentalism as a "liberal" cause. Some Christians and churches, in spite of overwhelming evidence to the contrary, still deny the reality of climate change. A Christian prophetic voice on this subject is badly needed, calling for responsible care of God's created order.

You might ask, "Is earth care really a spiritual concern? Does the Bible have anything to say about conservation of the natural order? Is there a theology of ecology?" The answer is yes. Several biblical principles about the environment follow.

A Theology of Ecology

1. God *created* the universe. "I am the LORD, the Maker of all things, who stretches out the heavens, who spreads out

the earth by myself" (Isa. 44:24). A theology of ecology must begin with God's creation of the universe.

2. God *affirms* God's creation. "God saw all that he had made, and it was very good" (Gen. 1:31).

3. God is *involved* in the creation. "You renew the face of the ground" (Ps. 104:30). This does not mean God operates levers and pulleys in heaven and says, "OK, I'll send some rain here, a tornado there, a hurricane over here, and an earthquake there." But the Bible is clear that God is mysteriously involved in creation. The changing of the seasons, the growth of crops, the renewal of life—all these happen because of God's ongoing involvement in creation.

4. God *cares* about all life on the planet. We know that God cares about people. But God also cares about other life. In Leviticus 25 God commanded the people not to overuse the land. God cares about topsoil and dirt. In Exodus 23 God told the people to treat animals with kindness. God cares about donkeys, oxen, horses, cats, dogs, and all animals. In Deuteronomy 20 we learn that even the trees have rights. I'm not saying we cannot ever cut down a tree. But the Bible teaches that God cares about all life on the planet, even plants and trees. Two chapters later, in Deuteronomy 22, God tells the people not to trap a bird when it is nesting its young. In short, God cares about birds, trees, animals, the land, and all life on the planet.

5. God desires *renewal* for creation. "The creation itself will be liberated from its bondage to decay" (Rom. 8:21). The earth is obviously incomplete and broken in many ways. But God is always working for renewal, and we can be a part of that renewal.

6. God *owns* all of creation. "The whole earth is mine" (Exod. 19:5). The planet is not ours to exploit. It belongs to God. And it's our job to care for it, which brings me to the final principle.

7. God appointed us as *stewards* of creation. "The LORD God took the man and put him in the Garden of Eden to

work it and take care of it" (Gen. 2:15). People of faith must be in the business of caring for the planet. God has called humans to tend the garden. As stewards of creation, we can do at least three things to help conserve God's creation.

First, we can change our life-style. The American way of life is hazardous to the health of our planet. As Christians who are concerned about conserving God's creation, we need to ask ourselves some hard questions about our materialistic value system. Dorothy Sayers once said, "A society in which consumption has to be artificially stimulated in order to keep production going is a society founded on trash and waste and such a society is a house built upon the sand."[2] Our worship of consumerism must end if we are to be responsible stewards of the earth. We must learn that bigger isn't always better, that a higher standard of living doesn't buy happiness, and that true peace and contentment come from a more simple life that does not take such a toll on the environment.

Numerous life-style changes by concerned Christians can help conserve God's creation, from carpooling or using mass transit, to recycling, to making our homes more energy efficient, to driving environmentally friendly vehicles. A few years ago a Christian advertising firm created a controversial ad campaign. It played off the popular phrase, "What would Jesus do?" However, in this case, the ad said, "What would Jesus drive?" The ad argued that given today's environmental problems, Jesus would drive an energy-efficient vehicle. It made some people mad, but it provoked an important debate. What *would* Jesus drive? It's not a bad question to ask. If we want to be good stewards of God's creation, we need to make some life-style changes that are less damaging to the earth.

Second, we can get politically involved as advocates for the earth. I'm not speaking of partisan politics but of good Christian citizenship. Environmental issues are constantly debated in government at the local, state, and national levels. Concerned Christians can advocate for responsible earth care to our elected officials, encouraging them to support laws that protect and conserve the environment.

Third, we can join others. Environmental problems cannot be solved on an individual level alone. People must work together in order to protect God's creation. Therefore, many concerned Christians have joined conservation groups in order to work with others to care for the earth. Numerous environmental groups exist, and we would do well to join one of them. Making life-style changes, getting politically involved, and joining others are just a few beginning steps, but they can make a real difference.

Excessive consumerism and environmental destruction are just two examples of twenty-first century prophetic concerns. American Christianity also needs to provide a prophetic voice in many other areas. For example, good religion needs to challenge "prosperity" religion, which promises that faithful believers will receive material blessings from God. This theology goes directly against the example and teaching of Jesus. The church also needs to offer a prophetic voice on important biblical issues like race relations, hunger, poverty, immigration, peacemaking, and radical individualism at the expense of the common good. Many other examples could be offered, but the point is simple: Good religion must constantly provide a prophetic voice in the culture.

Note

1. Jim Wallis, *God's Politics* (San Francisco: HarperSan-Francisco, 2005), 34–48.

2. Dorothy Sayers, *Creed or Chaos* (New York: Harcourt-Brace, 1949), 46, quoted in Henlee H. Barnette, *The Church and the Ecological Crisis* (Grand Rapids: Wm. B. Eerdmans Publishing Co., 1972), 47.

12

⨳

GOOD RELIGION BUILDS COMMUNITY

I once heard about a middle-aged atheist named Fred who regularly attended worship at a Jewish synagogue. Finally someone got up the nerve to ask him about this. "Fred, everyone here knows you don't believe in God. So we can't help but wonder — why do you come to worship every week? We're glad you are here, but it's a bit confusing."

Fred smiled and pointed to a man across the room. He said, "Do you see Mr. Simon over there? Mr. Simon comes to worship every week to talk to God. I come to worship every week to talk to Mr. Simon."

As a pastor I hope people come to church to talk to God. But I also hope they come to church to talk and connect with other human begins. Why? Because building friendships and community is a crucial part of healthy religion.

We, Not Me

Like many churches around the world, my congregation prays the Lord's Prayer at almost every worship service. Many people, even nonreligious persons, are familiar with this prayer. Note that the Lord's Prayer doesn't say, "*My* father." Instead it says, "*Our* father." The prayer doesn't say, "Give *me my* daily bread." Instead it says, "Give *us our* daily bread." The prayer doesn't say, "Forgive *me my* trespasses." Instead it says, "Forgive *us our* trespasses." On nine occasions the Lord's Prayer uses the terms "our," "us," and "we." Perhaps it would be helpful to see what I'm talking about. The Lord's Prayer follows, with an emphasis on the community connections:

> OUR Father, who art in heaven, hallowed be thy name. Thy kingdom come, thy will be done, on earth as it is in heaven. Give US this day OUR daily bread. And forgive US OUR trespasses, as WE forgive those who trespass against US. And lead US not into temptation, but deliver US from evil. For thine is the kingdom and the power and the glory forever, amen.

Christianity is not an individual religion. It's a *community* religion. You and I can't be Christians in isolation. We can be Christians only in relationships with other Christians.

A Presbyterian pastor once received a complaint from a guest who visited his church. This church, like many others, has a time in the worship service for "passing the peace." This ancient tradition goes back to the early church in the New Testament. During the passing of the peace, people greet one another in Christian love and friendship. People say to those around them, "The peace of Christ be with you," and people respond, "And also with you." During the passing of the peace, people often shake hands and sometimes hug one another. The passing of the peace is a way of saying, "We come to worship not only as individuals but also as a community of faith, as a church family."

This visitor at that Presbyterian church did not like passing the peace. He said to the pastor, "The passing of the peace feels like an invasion of my privacy."

The pastor replied, "When you come to church, to some extent you give up some of your privacy." This pastor was exactly right. Church is not a private affair. Christianity is not an individualistic religion. It's a community religion. Christianity is a *we* faith, not a *me* faith.

A "One Another" Church

The concept of Christian friendship and community is a crucial teaching of the Bible. For example, over and over again in the New Testament, you find the phrase "one another." A few examples follow:

— "Love one another." (John 13:34)
— "Accept one another." (Rom. 15:7)
— "Teach . . . one another." (Col. 3:16)
— "Greet one another." (1 Cor. 16:20)
— "Serve one another." (Gal. 5:13)
— "Be kind and compassionate to one another." (Eph. 4:32)
— "Be patient, bearing with one another." (Eph. 4:2)
— "Forgive one another." (Col. 3:13)
— "Encourage one another." (1 Thess. 5:11)
— "Pray for one another." (Jas. 5:16 NRSV)

The New Testament has at least fifty "one another" verses. The Bible is clear. We are part of a "one another" religion. I don't want to overromanticize this notion. It doesn't mean we always get along perfectly. It doesn't even mean that we all have to like one another. Do you get along perfectly and like everyone in your extended family? I doubt it. So this "one another" theme of the Bible is not some kind of idealistic, warm and fuzzy church where people never disagree or have conflict. But it does mean that we are all part of God's family, connected to one another by our common faith in Jesus Christ, and that we live out our faith not as individual believers but together as a community of faith.

One of the deepest needs we have in life is the need to connect with other people. Human beings crave connection—we are wired for community. We see that truth throughout the Bible. Genesis 2 says, "It is not good for the man to be alone" (v. 18). From the beginning God created us for connection with others. Ecclesiastes 4:9 says, "Two are better than one." The text goes on to say that we cannot survive the obstacles of life without the help of friends. Proverbs 15:22 says, "Plans fail for lack of counsel, but with many advisers they succeed." In other words, when we make plans and decisions, we need the advice of friends. Romans 12:15 says, "Rejoice with those who rejoice, weep with those who weep" (NRSV). Everyone needs friends they can laugh and cry with. And Galatians 6:2 says, "Carry each other's burdens." Life is hard sometimes, and we need others to help us carry the load. In short, God calls Christian believers to connect, love, and support one another as we love and serve God and neighbor.

Although many ways exist to form Christian friendships, two ways to develop a supportive faith community are to connect with a local church through worship and to connect to individuals through small groups. Gathering with the community of faith every Sunday for worship is at the core of our faith. It's crucial that we sing together, pray together, pass the peace together, hear God's Word together, and celebrate Holy Communion together. Worship builds Christian community.

A second way to form Christian community is to participate in a small group in your congregation, like a Bible study group, a Sunday school class, a music group, a men's or women's group, or a service group of some kind. Small-group life is not always easy. Some members of your group might be obnoxious. Some of the lessons might be boring. Conflict occasionally occurs. You won't always agree. But connecting together as the people of God on a journey together to grow spiritually, to support one another, and to love and serve God and neighbor is at the heart of Christianity. This kind of small-group faith community goes all the way back to Jesus. In Mark 3 we learn that Jesus appointed twelve disciples "that they might be with him" (v. 14). Jesus formed a group of twelve disciples to be together, learn together, worship together, serve together, and support one another. Christianity literally began as a small-group movement.

More Than a List

One of my favorite passages in the Bible is Romans 16:1–16. If you read this text, the previous sentence will probably puzzle you. Romans 16 is nothing more than a long list of names, hard-to-pronounce names at that. They are the names of people who belonged to the church of Rome in Paul's day. It's a pretty boring passage to read. But Paul would be offended if you referred to it as a mere list. It was far more than that to him. These were people who helped Paul through some hard times in his life and people he dearly loved.

In verse 3 we read about Aquila and Priscilla. They risked their necks for Paul. In verse 5 Paul speaks of his dear friend Epenetus, his first convert in Asia. He tells about Mary, who worked hard for the Lord, in verse 6. In verse 7 he lists Andronicus and Junia, who spent time in prison with Paul for proclaiming the gospel. Paul speaks of his dear friend Stachys in verse 9. In verse 12 he mentions his close friend Persis, and in verse 13 he lists Rufus and Rufus's mother, who was like a mother to him. Can you imagine a women being like a mother to Paul? I can almost hear her say, "Now, Paul, I don't care if you are an apostle, you have to eat your vegetables!"

This list has many names. But it is far more than a list to Paul. These people meant the world to him. The fact is, everybody needs a list. One of the primary purposes of good religion is to provide close relationships. Authentic Christianity builds lists.

I remember Carol's list. Carol was a member of a church I used to serve. Carol is a wonderful woman, full of life and joy. But years ago Carol's teenage son was killed in a car wreck. About six or eight weeks after his death, Carol brought an article to me at the church office to be published in the church newsletter. It was basically a list of names. She wanted to thank some people in the church for their support during that horrible time. People like Susan, who came right over and answered the phone and called relatives and friends with the bad news. And Judy, who stayed at Carol's house for almost a week, cleaning house and cooking and keeping things going. And Charles, who came over and mowed the lawn for several months after the death. And Jo, who also lost a son a few years earlier. Jo came and sat and cried with Carol. She understood.

"Thank you," said Carol to these people and several others. It was just a list of names. It would not be interesting if you were reading the church newsletter and didn't know who these people were or what they did. But to Carol it was far more than a list. It was the names of the people who helped her survive the worst nightmare of her life. They have a name for that sort of thing back where I come from. They call it "church family." Indeed, Carol began her list by saying, "Dear Church Family."

What Attracted You to This Church?

I once attended a church leadership conference led by Lyle Schaller, a well-known church consultant and author. Years ago Schaller did consulting work for a church in Minneapolis. As part of his consultation he visited the Sunday morning worship service. After the service was over, he asked a few of the members why they attended that church. He asked the question of a young woman in her mid-thirties named Jennifer.

Lyle asked her, "What attracted you to this church?"

Jennifer said, "Do you really want to know?"

He said, "Yes." So, for the next thirty minutes, Jennifer told her story.

Jennifer had been successful in her career, was married, and hoped to have children. However, like many young people, she felt restless and had no real meaning in her life. So she began to experiment with cocaine. At first it was just for kicks. In time, however, she was seriously hooked on the drug. Through her addiction she lost her husband, she lost most of her resources, she lost her self-dignity, and she was close to losing her job.

Jennifer lived in a downtown apartment complex, right next to a church. One day she walked past the church, as she had done many times before. As she passed the front entrance, a young woman walked out the door of the church, carrying a baby. The woman saw Jennifer and said hello. They both stopped for a moment while Jennifer admired the baby. The woman asked Jennifer, "Do you live around here?" Jennifer told her she lived in the high-rise apartment building right next to the church. After some small talk, the woman asked Jennifer if she went to church anywhere. Jennifer said no. The woman said, "We'd love to have you visit our church sometime." She wasn't pushy. She just offered a simple invitation. They ended their conversation, and Jennifer went home.

Over the next few days, Jennifer could not forget the encounter with the woman from the church. She seemed like such a nice person, a person Jennifer would like to know, a person Jennifer would like to be like. She told her coworker about the incident, and her colleague said, "Maybe you ought to go visit the church."

Jennifer said, "Maybe I will."

Two weeks later Jennifer showed up at the church, feeling scared and awkward. She had not been to church for over a decade. The young woman who invited Jennifer to visit the church saw her walk through the front door. She walked up to Jennifer and gave her a warm welcome. She invited Jennifer to sit by her during the service. After worship they went to lunch together. Over the next couple of months, these two women developed a friendship. In time, Jennifer admitted to this woman that she had a drug problem.

The woman said, "Why don't you come to the Winners' Club at our church?"

"The what?" Jennifer asked.

"The Winners' Club," she repeated. Then she explained that the Winner's Club was a twelve-step, small-group program to help people get off drugs. Jennifer went to the Winner's Club. By the grace of God, the help of the twelve-step small group, and the love and support of that church, she got off drugs and got her life back. One year later, in a Sunday morning worship service, the pastor, who knew Jennifer's story, said to the congregation—with Jennifer's permission — "We have a birthday today. Jennifer has been drug-free for one year today." Spontaneously, the congregation stood up and sang "Happy Birthday." Afterward dozens of people came up to Jennifer and hugged her and told her how proud they were of her.

Jennifer then looked at Lyle Schaller, the consultant interviewing her. She said, "In a few weeks, I'll be off drugs for two years, and my church promised to sing 'Happy Birthday' to me again." She concluded her story by saying, "This congregation invited me to church, and when I came, full of fear, they welcomed me. In spite of my drug problem, they loved me and supported me. They helped me connect with God and became my family. And that, Mr. Schaller, is why I come to this church."

13

❦

GOOD RELIGION
IS HOPE FILLED

I once heard a story about a group of Jews living in a large Jewish ghetto during World War II. I don't know if the story is historical or fictional, but either way it's a story full of truth. The ghettos of WWII were not as bad as the concentration camps, but they were close. The people had a few more freedoms than they did in the camps, but they were still prisoners. With German guards all around, nobody could come in or out. For years they lived in the ghetto, just barely surviving, with no news about the war's progress. After years of struggle, they finally ran out of hope. As a result, about two or three people committed suicide every day. Then something happened to change all of that.

One day a man from the ghetto named Jacob got in trouble and was arrested by a soldier. He got caught on the street past curfew, so he was taken to see a German officer. While waiting to talk to the captain for his infraction, he overheard a radio news report. The report said Allied troops were marching through Germany. Jacob realized the Germans were near defeat. Even more exciting, he learned that the Allied troops were not far from the Jewish ghetto where he lived and were moving in that direction. This news filled Jacob with great hope—hope that the Germans might be defeated, hope that he and his community would soon be delivered from the ghetto. Once he returned to the ghetto, his exhilarating news spread rapidly, giving the people renewed hope. That hope transformed them. Once again people began to laugh, and young couples began to make wedding plans. Most telling, the daily suicides came to a complete halt.

Hope impacts the human spirit in remarkable ways. And hope is a core characteristic of healthy religion. In fact, hope is at the heart of the Christian faith.

We Lived on Hope

Not long ago I watched a retired veteran interviewed on public television. Back in the 1960s his airplane crashed over Vietnam, the crew was captured, and he became a Vietnam prisoner of war. During the interview he told about his awful experience as a POW. The interviewer asked him, "How did you and your comrades make it through those difficult years?"

His response caught my attention. He said, "We lived on hope." Some of their hopes were small. Hope they would not be beaten that day. Hope that dinner rations would be a little bigger than usual. Of course, their biggest hope was that the war would end and they could go home again. Since watching that interview I've thought a lot about his comment: "We lived on hope." His words made me realize that *everyone*, in one way or another, lives on hope. Without hope we could not survive. Hope is one of the most important forces in human life.

I once heard about a physical therapist who works with spinal cord injury patients. At the time one of his patients was a sixteen-year-old boy who had obtained his driver's license nine months earlier. A few months after receiving his license he severed his spine in a gymnastics drill, paralyzing him from the waist down. For a while the boy felt depressed and hopeless. But the physical therapist told the boy that if he wanted, he could learn to drive again. In fact, the therapist told the boy that the rehab unit had a section that taught paralyzed people to drive using only their hands.

The boy said to the physical therapist, "You really think I can drive a car again?"

The therapist said, "Yes, I believe you can."

When the boy heard those words, his eyes begin to glisten. He saw a flicker of hope. A few minutes later the boy pulled himself out of his bed and got into his wheelchair. He asked the physical therapist to take him to the lab where they taught paralyzed people how to drive again. So they went. The therapist said the boy stared silently at the car for almost twenty minutes. He sensed a great debate going on in his mind as to whether he could ever drive again. The next morning the boy came by the therapist's office and said, "I want to start learning to drive as soon as possible."

The physical therapist said, "At that point I knew he would make it."

Other than love, hope is the most powerful force on earth. And God is the author of hope. Hope is one of the greatest gifts God ever gave his creation. The Bible is full of passages on hope. For example, Romans 15:13 says, "May the God of hope fill you with all joy and peace as you trust in him, so that you may overflow with hope by the power of the Holy Spirit." Proverbs 23:18 says, "There is surely a future hope for you, and your hope will not be cut off." Hebrews 6:19 says, "We have this hope as an anchor for the soul, firm and secure." Hope is at the center of the gospel. And it's rooted in the resurrection of Jesus Christ.

Think about the resurrection for a moment. Evil had done its most devious work. Jesus had been rejected, abandoned, put on trial, mocked, beaten, and crucified until he died. His followers placed his lifeless body in a tomb. It seemed like evil had finally prevailed. The followers of Christ felt devastated. All hope was gone. They hid from the authorities, fearful for their own lives. But on the third day, on Easter Sunday, God said, "Death shall not prevail, and evil shall not win." And God raised Jesus from the dead. The resurrection of Jesus gives us hope for life and even hope for death. The empty tomb of Easter gives us hope for physical death. As Paul said in 1 Corinthians 15, "Where, O death, is your victory? Where, O death, is your sting? . . . But thanks be to God! He gives us the victory through our Lord Jesus Christ" (vv. 55, 57). Hope in the face of death is a rich gift from God.

However, many other kinds of death besides physical death exist in the world. For example, the death of a dream, the death of a marriage, the death of a job, the death of a friendship, and the death of good health. In all these circumstances, we have hope for a better tomorrow because we belong to a God of resurrection, a God who brings life out of death—every kind of death.

Tell Us a Resurrection Story

A few years ago I heard a story about a clergywoman named Barbara Brown Taylor. Barbara, an Episcopal priest, now serves as a college professor. When she served as a parish priest, every month, on a Monday afternoon, Barbara drove to a nursing home to lead worship and serve Communion to the residents. It was not her favorite pastoral duty. Many of the residents were seriously ill. Some slept during the service. Some were confused. Some suffered from dementia and said and did strange things. I can tell you from personal experience that leading a worship service at a nursing home is hard pastoral duty. But people in nursing homes matter to God, and they matter to God's church. So once a month Barbara went to the nursing home to lead worship and serve Communion.

One Monday afternoon, when Barbara was leading the worship service, a confused woman began singing, "Row, row, row your boat!" It distracted everyone.

In an effort to gain their attention, Barbara clapped her hands and said, "What story from the Bible shall I read to you this afternoon? What part of the Bible would you like to hear?"

Things got quiet for a moment. Then an old woman's broken voice said, "Tell us a resurrection story."

A moment of silence followed. Then another resident said, "Yes, tell us a resurrection story."

Before long, almost all of them were saying, "Tell us a resurrection story."

The crowd at that nursing home held no illusions about themselves. They knew they were old, poor, broken, fragile, and had little time left. So in their great need and in their great hope, they said, "Tell us a resurrection story."

Most of you reading this book are not like those people in that nursing home. Most of you are not in walkers or wheelchairs, nor do you suffer from dementia. On the contrary you might be healthy, live in a lovely home, drive a nice car, and have a good job with a generous 401(k). Yet all of us, if we are honest, are not very different from the people in that nursing home. In many ways we, like them, are broken, frail, confused, and anxious. Like them we need a resurrection story. I'd like to tell you one of my favorites.

Are We Having Easter This Year?

Back in March 1994 a young woman named Kelly Clem served as pastor of Goshen United Methodist Church in Piedmont, Alabama. The Sunday before Easter, on Palm Sunday, the congregation packed the church. Kelly placed her two-year-old daughter, Sarah, in the church nursery. Kelly's four-year-old daughter, Hannah, dressed in a little blue-and-white choir robe, sat on the front pew with the children's choir. As the service got under way, the congregation heard wind blowing outside. The sky turned black. Then the lightning began, followed by hail. Suddenly a burst of wind hit the building. The stained-glass window shattered, and shards of glass shot across the sanctuary. Somebody shouted, "Tornado!" Pieces of ceiling started to fall. A horrible sound followed as the roof of the church ripped off and the building crashed around them.

Reverend Kelly ran to check on her children, but a brick hit her on the head and she fell hard on her shoulder. When she finally got up, she looked around at the devastation. Someone told her that her two-year-old daughter, Sarah, was OK—that the nursery was still intact. Then Kelly looked at where her four-year-old daughter, Hannah, had been sitting. The area was covered by a pile of bricks. Underneath that pile of bricks she could see little blue-and-white choir robes. Members of the church pulled Hannah and the other children out of the bricks, but Hannah did not make it. Nineteen people died that day, and eighty-six others were injured. The days that followed were brutal. Kelly performed one funeral after another, including a funeral for her own daughter. Toward the end of that devastating week, Kelly began to get phone calls from members of the congregation. They asked the strangest question. "Reverend Clem," they asked, "are we having Easter this year?"

Kelly knew they weren't just asking about Sunday's services. She knew they were saying, "Reverend Clem, we desperately *need* Easter." And after officiating at multiple funerals, including the funeral of her four-year-old daughter, Kelly Clem knew *she* needed Easter, too. So Kelly and her congregation planned an Easter sunrise service. The church had been destroyed, so they had the service out on the lawn, in the midst of all the devastation of the tornado. Early on Easter morning, more than two hundred people gathered on the front yard of the church. There, in that dismal setting of destruction and death, Reverend Kelly Clem, with a bandage on her head and her shoulder in a brace, made her way to the makeshift pulpit. She looked into the faces of people whose dreams and lives had been shattered. Then she read the words of the apostle Paul in Romans 8, "For I am convinced that neither death nor life . . . nor anything else in all creation, will be able to separate us from the love of God that is in Christ Jesus our Lord" (vv. 38–39). And with those words the Goshen United Methodist Church of Piedmont, Alabama, began their Easter service. They sang "Christ the Lord Is Risen Today." They read the Easter story about how God brings life even out of death. They prayed.

Many years have passed since that sunrise Easter worship service at the Goshen church. But that Easter hope—hope that God brings life even out of destruction and death—gave the people of Goshen United Methodist Church in Piedmont, Alabama, the strength to rebuild their church. And that Easter resurrection hope gave Reverend Kelly Clem and her family the strength to rebuild their lives. The day after the tornado a reporter asked Reverend Clem if the disaster had shattered her faith.

She replied, "It has not shattered my faith. I'm holding on to my faith. It's holding me. All of the people of Goshen are holding on to each other, along with the hope they will be able to rebuild." Then Kelly, physically injured and full of grief over the death of her daughter, said to the reporter, "Easter is coming."

And Easter came, both for Kelly and for her church. With God's help the good people of Goshen UMC did rebuild their church and their lives. And so did Kelly Clem and her family. Since the tornado, Kelly and her husband, Dale, have continued to live life with faith and hope. And they have continued to serve God and God's church. Several years after the tornado, Kelly and Dale had another child, a little girl named Laurel. After serving as United Methodist missionaries in Lithuania, Kelly and her husband returned to Alabama and are currently living full lives and serving churches in Huntsville. Such is the power of Easter resurrection hope—hope for life and hope for death.

It's Empty

About fifteen years ago I made a trip to Israel, what Christians often call "the Holy Land." My group went to see many important places. We went to the Sea of Galilee, where Jesus taught and sometimes fished with his disciples. We also went to Bethlehem, where Jesus was born. We visited all kinds of places from the stories of the Bible. But the most sacred place we visited was the garden tomb, the place we believe Jesus was buried. I could tell you a lot of things about the garden tomb. It's surrounded by beautiful plants and flowers. Right across from the tomb, there's a small amphitheater where groups can worship. My group celebrated Communion there. It's probably the most meaningful Communion service I've ever experienced. I could tell you other interesting things about this sacred place. But really, there's only one thing you need to know about the garden tomb.

It's empty.

14

GOOD RELIGION KEEPS AN OPEN MIND

I once saw a poster with an image of Jesus on it. The caption said, "He died to take away your sins. Not your mind."

One characteristic of good religion is that it keeps an open mind. People of faith need to be willing to ask hard questions, to grapple with our faith, to debate, to think. The motto of my denomination, the United Methodist Church is, "Open Hearts, Open Minds, and Open Doors." The church of Jesus Christ should always be a church of open minds. That's certainly the spirit of Jesus. In the Great Commandment, which we examined earlier, Jesus told us to love God "with all your *mind*" (Mark 12:30). In the book of Isaiah, the prophet says, "Come now, and let us *reason* together, says the LORD" (Isa. 1:18 NKJV). John Wesley, the founder of the Methodist Church once said, "But as to all opinions which do not strike at the root of Christianity, we *think and let think*."

Christians obviously have some nonnegotiables, primarily around the life, death, and resurrection of Jesus Christ. To be open-minded doesn't mean we don't have core convictions, values, beliefs, and practices—because we do. I recently received an e-mail from a pastor who read my previous book. He said, "Your book is a splendid description of a faith that is open-minded but not so open that one's brains fall out." I liked that quote. He was saying that a combination of foundational beliefs, along with an open mind, is a good recipe for faith. But beyond our core beliefs, we can grapple, debate, and even disagree on our theology. In the words of Jesus, we can love God with our mind. In the words of Isaiah, we can reason together. And in the words of John Wesley, we can think and let think.

The reason it's so important to keep an open mind is that we, unlike God, are not all knowing. Our understanding of God and faith is limited. No matter how hard we try, we will never fully comprehend the mysteries of life, faith, and God.

How Do You Draw God?

A couple of years ago, at a Sunday school party, we played an old but still fun game called Pictionary. If you are not familiar with this game, it's like charades, except instead of acting out a topic, you have to draw it. Since this was a church event, we added some religious terms just for fun. One lucky soul got "Nebuchadnezzar." A man named Gary drew a card that said "son of God." He got "son" easily enough. He drew a large stick man and then a little one, and immediately a team member said, "son." But Gary felt completely stumped on "God." He tried all sorts of images. But in the end nobody guessed that he was trying to draw God. After the timer went off, Gary said, exasperated, "How in the world do you draw God?"

We can't draw God. Nor can we adequately describe God. Nor can we find absolute and perfect answers to every question about God and faith. Authentic Christianity needs to have some theological modesty. Every detail about Christianity is not completely clear. Some things are always going to be unresolved.

Many of you are familiar with Garrison Keillor. He broadcasts a radio show on public radio every Saturday night called *A Prairie Home Companion*. The highlight of his weekly radio show is a story from the fictional town of Lake Wobegon, Minnesota. Every week he ends the story by saying, "And that's the news from Lake Wobegon, where all the women are strong, all the men are good-looking, and all the children are above average."

A few years ago Keillor told a story about a mother who had a high school son. Her son and his friends had just waited in a long line all night long to buy tickets for an upcoming rock concert. A few days later this mother read an alarming article about that rock group. The article talked about how awful their songs are, how they encouraged drug use, and how horrible an influence they were on American young people. After reading the article, she went to her son's room and found the tickets to that rock concert. She took out a cigarette lighter and wondered, "Should I burn these tickets or not?" She went back and forth, debating the decision. And with that, Garrison Keillor ended the story. He said, "And that's the news from Lake Wobegon, where all the women are strong, all the men are good-looking, and all the children are above average."

On his next show Garrison Keillor said he received large numbers of e-mails and letters that week from listeners who felt frustrated that he left them hanging, that he left the story unresolved. Then he said, "I don't know about your life, but in my life, a lot of things are left unresolved."

Garrison Keillor is right, of course. Life is often unresolved. Many things are left hanging. Life has many unanswered questions. We don't always see things clearly. Life is not always neat and resolved. Instead, life is often ambiguous and unresolved. And the same dynamic is true with faith. Therefore, authentic Christianity needs to have some theological modesty. In short, we need to keep an open mind because we are not all knowing.

"If You Fight Science, You Are Going to Lose Your Children"

Take creation, for example. Nobody knows for sure how God created the world. But some Christians claim to know all the details. A conservative group of Christians, called "young earth creationists," claim the earth is only six thousand to ten thousand years old. They base that belief on an extremely literal reading of Genesis, and they insist that all Bible-believing Christians agree with them. But even Pat Robertson, a fundamentalist religious-right leader, doubts that claim. In an episode of his TV show, *The 700 Club*, Robertson questioned this "young earth" theology. He said, "There was a time when these giant reptiles [dinosaurs] were on the earth, and it was before the time of the Bible. So don't try and cover it up and make like everything was six thousand years. That's not the Bible." However, the more important comment he made that day on the air came later in the conversation when he said, "If you fight science, you are going to lose your children."

I rarely agree with Pat Robertson. But on this topic I could not agree more. Science tells us that the earth is about 4.5 billion years old. As Bill Nye, "The Science Guy," says, "And if that conflicts with your beliefs, I strongly feel you should question your beliefs." He's exactly right. If we force young people to choose between science and faith, we are going to lose a lot of people to the Christian faith, both young and old. As John Pierce said in an editorial of *Baptists Today*, "When Christianity gets reduced to, and presented as, a firm checklist of beliefs that includes such matters as literal interpretations of the ancient biblical story and narrow political ideologies, many young people will simply check out—and, frankly, others who are not-so-young will, too."[1]

The Wesleyan Quadrilateral

Christians need to keep an open mind because we'll never fully understand every dimension of religious belief and practice. Therefore, we need to be open to various opinions and beliefs. However, that does not mean we don't have tools for thinking carefully about our faith. The United Methodist Church, for example, has a theological process for thinking about faith called "the Wesleyan Quadrilateral." Although our founder, John Wesley, never used that term, he used the process in his theological thinking. Our affirmation of the Wesleyan Quadrilateral means we have four sources of theological authority: Scripture, tradition, experience, and reason. To illustrate how this works, let me tell you how we used the quadrilateral to affirm that women can serve as clergy.

First, our church looked at *Scripture*. The truth is, when it comes to women in ministry, Scripture is a mixed bag. Some passages affirm women in church leadership and even mention women preaching. However, a few passages in the Bible are negative about women being pastors, which can easily be explained by the historical context behind those passages.

Second, we looked at *tradition*. Just like Scripture, tradition is mixed. During the first few centuries of the church, women served in many leadership roles, including preaching and pastoral roles. But then, for many centuries, women were mostly excluded from leadership. However, in the past few centuries, women have played major roles in church ministry. So, like Scripture, tradition is a mixed bag.

Next, we looked at *experience*. That was much easier to sort out. Our experience teaches us that women clearly have the gifts to be effective ministers. Some of our best pastors are female.

Finally, we looked at *reason*. Reason tells us that women, like men, are created in the image of God, fully equal with men and fully capable of being ministers in the church.

So the United Methodist Church, like most other mainline denominations, grappled with Scripture, tradition, experience, and reason and then said, we believe women can and should serve as clergy. And the church has been deeply blessed by that decision. You might be interested to know that there are more women ministers in my denomination than any other denomination in the world. Why? Because we, along with other moderate and mainline denominations, attempt to be Christian believers with open minds. I recommend that you do the same.

Note

1. John Pierce, "Pat Got It Right This Time, Will We?" *Baptists Today*, January 2013, 7.

15

⌘

GOOD RELIGION
PRACTICES FORGIVENESS

A middle-aged United Methodist minister owned a bright red 1967 Ford Mustang. He completely restored it to mint condition; it was absolutely immaculate, and it was his pride and joy. This minister also had a teen-age son, and it was almost time for his son's senior prom. The boy begged his dad to let him drive the Mustang to his prom. At first the preacher said no, worried that his son might damage his beloved car. But finally he gave in. The boy promised to drive carefully, to drive slowly, and to park it away from other cars so it would not get dinged.

At 11 p.m. on the night of the prom, the minister received a phone call from his son. "Dad," he said, "my date and I are OK, but I've had a minor accident in your car."

The pastor and his wife rushed to the scene, and when he arrived, his heart sank. One whole side of his beautiful Mustang was smashed in. Outraged, he began to tear into his son. His wife, however, said, "Now, honey, you need to forgive him."

"But my Mustang," he replied.

"Now, honey," she continued, "you tell the people at our church all the time that they must forgive the sins of others."

"But my Mustang," he said.

Finally, she said, "Now, honey, as you always say, 'To err is human—to forgive divine.'"

The pastor said, "That's true, it is divine to forgive. But God doesn't own a *fully restored 1967 Mustang!*"

Forgiveness does not come easy for most people. But forgiveness is a core characteristic of good religion. In fact, forgiveness was a favorite topic for Jesus. You might say Jesus was in the forgiveness business. He constantly served as a bearer of grace and forgiveness. Everywhere you look in the New Testament, Jesus forgives someone. Throughout his ministry Jesus associated with sinners, and he treated them with amnesty, offering them the gift of grace and forgiveness. Even during his crucifixion, Jesus was in the forgiveness business. As the soldiers executed him and the crowd jeered at him, he said, "Father, forgive them, for they do not know what they are doing" (Luke 23:34). Jesus' entire ministry revolved around forgiveness.

Forgive Us Our Trespasses

We see that vividly in the Lord's Prayer. In this prayer Jesus taught his disciples to pray, "Forgive us our trespasses as we forgive those who trespass against us." Jesus clearly teaches us that when we pray, we need to ask God to forgive our sins. The fact is, all of us need to be forgiven over and over again: forgiven for words spoken in anger, forgiven for people we have hurt, forgiven for the chances we have missed and the years we have wasted, forgiven for moral failures. We are sinners, every one, and we need to be forgiven. So Jesus teaches us to pray, "Forgive us our sins." And like a good and loving parent, God forgives us.

When I was a young boy I learned a vivid lesson in forgiveness from my mother. However, it didn't start out that way. My mother was so angry at me that she was speechless. The drive home was unbearably long. The first item on the agenda was the hairbrush. Spankings with the hairbrush were reserved only for the most serious infractions. After the spanking I was sent to my room. Now that I am a parent, I understand the ritual of sending children to their rooms. It's a good way to stall for time when parents cannot figure out what to do with their kids!

What happened to put me in this predicament? Influenced by peer pressure I had been stealing from a local dime store. No grand larceny, mind you, but stealing all the same. I had stolen a candy bar one day, an inexpensive toy the next, and so on. That day it was a plastic ring. It cost only a dime, and I had a dollar in my pocket, but an eight-year-old boy will do foolish things to impress his friends and to feel he belongs to the group.

At the moment I slipped the ring into my pocket, the store manager abruptly grabbed me and demanded my name and phone number. My mother arrived shortly, embarrassed and livid with anger. I felt ashamed. It was one of the most traumatic experiences of my brief eight years. As I sat in my room crying, I felt an awesome sense of guilt. For the first time in my life I doubted my mother's love for me. I felt I had done something so awful, so terrible, that she would no longer love me. I picked up a pencil and a Big Chief writing pad and wrote my mother a note saying, "Mommy. I'm sorry. Do you still love me?" Transporting the message, however, was a problem. I was upstairs, and Mom was downstairs. Finally, I came up with an ingenious plan. I folded the note into a paper airplane, opened my door, and sailed the message of repentance down the stairs.

Soon my mother came into my room. She had been crying. She walked to my bed, looked at me, and began to weep. Then she took me in her arms and said, "Yes, honey, I still love you. I love you more than anything in the world." As we embraced I felt a sense of love and forgiveness that I will never forget.

Like my mother on that day, God stands ready to forgive us when we fail. It's called "grace," and it's one of the best gifts God gives to God's children. As 1 John 1:9 says, "If we confess our sins, he is faithful and just and will forgive us our sins and purify us from all unrighteousness."

As We Forgive Those
Who Trespass against Us

When Jesus taught his followers to pray, "Forgive us our trespasses," he affirmed that God, in God's mercy, forgives our sins. But that's only one half of the prayer. Jesus immediately adds, "As we forgive those who trespass against us."

Jesus is telling us something important here. He says, since God has forgiven our sins, we need to forgive the sins of others. In fact, right after Jesus taught his disciples the Lord's Prayer, he added these words: "For if you forgive others their trespasses, your heavenly Father will also forgive you; but if you do not forgive others, neither will your Father forgive your trespasses" (Matt. 6:14–15 NRSV). Over and over again Jesus said, "Since we have received God's forgiveness, we must give forgiveness to others." That's the deal. We don't just see this in the Lord's Prayer. We see it throughout the Bible. Several examples follow:

— "Forgive, and you will be forgiven." (Luke 6:37)
— "Forgiving each other, just as in Christ God forgave you." (Eph. 4:32)

— "Forgive one another if any of you has a grievance against someone. Forgive as the Lord forgave you." (Col. 3:13)
— "Peter came to Jesus and asked, 'Lord, how many times shall I forgive my brother or sister who sins against me? Up to seven times?' Jesus answered, 'I tell you, not seven times, but seventy-seven times.'" (Matt. 18:21–22)
— "And when you stand praying, if you hold anything against anyone, forgive them, so that your Father in heaven may forgive you your sins." (Mark 11:25)

Accepting God's forgiveness is liberating and joyful. However, forgiving others is harder. Forgiving people who have wronged us is no easy task: the parent who wounded us, the child who failed us, the coworker who stabbed us in the back, the fellow church member who hurt our feelings, the spouse who disappointed us. Yet Jesus said we must forgive these people, just as God has forgiven us. And it's not just a suggestion; it's a command. Why is that? Why was Jesus so adamant about forgiving people? Many reasons could be listed. We forgive because God forgives. We forgive because Jesus commands us to forgive. We forgive because people desperately need to be forgiven. But Jesus also wants us to forgive others because we *need* to forgive.

"It Beats Tranquilizers All to Pieces!"

I used to think forgiveness was primarily for the benefit of the person being forgiven, and there is some truth to that. When people sin, they need to be forgiven, to be absolved of their sin. But after three decades in ministry I've come to realize that forgiveness benefits the person who forgives even more than it benefits the person who is forgiven. It's like the divorced woman who, for years, nursed bitterness against her unfaithful ex-husband. But over time, keeping that anger, hostility, and bitterness alive became a cancer in her mind and body and soul. Finally, for her own physical, emotional, and spiritual health, she decided to forgive him, even though he didn't ask for it or deserve it. Several months later she told her pastor that forgiving her ex-husband felt like taking a one-hundred-pound weight off her chest. She said, "I can sleep again. I can smile again. I can laugh again. I can live again. It beats tranquilizers all to pieces." Forgiving others is one of the most liberating actions we can ever take.

"If I Continued to Hate These People, I Was Still in Prison"

Most of you know the story of Nelson Mandela. He was imprisoned twenty-seven years for opposing the evil government of apartheid in South Africa. When the government released Mandela, he could have easily been bitter toward those who imprisoned him. But instead Mandela chose to forgive them. Former President Bill Clinton once asked Nelson Mandela how he was able to bring himself to forgive his jailers. Mandela said, "When I walked out of the gate, I knew that if I continued to hate these people, I was still in prison." Mandela realized that if he wanted to be free, he had to forgive.

Years ago, when I pastored a church in another state, I once preached a sermon on the healing power of forgiveness. A few days later a member of my congregation, a man in his forties, came to visit me. This man was carrying a lot of baggage concerning his father, who struggled with alcoholism. When he was a little boy, his dad used to slap him around. When he was a teenager, his dad humiliated him over and over again. His dad never showed him any love and never affirmed anything he did. And his dad was often mean to his mother. As a result, this man carried around a lot of anger and bitterness toward his father, and he had been doing so for a long time. He knew his bitterness toward his father was hurting him in many ways, and he wanted to be free from it. After years of nursing anger and bitterness, he finally decided to forgive his dad.

How Do I Forgive a Dead Man?

However, about that same time, his father died. He thought his anger and bitterness would go away upon his dad's death, but it did not. So he came to me and asked, "How do I forgive a dead man?" We talked a long time. Finally, I suggested that he write a letter to his dad. He said, "What's the point? He's dead."

I said, "The letter is not for your dad; it's for you." I encouraged him to articulate in the letter, in detail, how his father had hurt him. But then I challenged him to clearly communicate his forgiveness.

He agreed to write the letter and worked on it for many weeks. It proved to be cathartic for him. In the letter he expressed how much his father had wounded him. But the letter also expressed his forgiveness. He listed, one by one, the things for which he forgave his father. Writing the letter was a powerful experience for this man. He shared the letter with me, and I was deeply moved. But that's not the end of the story.

A few weeks after he wrote the letter, this man went to his father's grave. He took out the letter and slowly and carefully read it out loud. "Dad, I forgive you for being an alcoholic. I forgive you for repeatedly slapping me. I forgive you for humiliating me. I forgive you for never saying you love me. I forgive you for your awful treatment of Mom." This went on for some time. With tears flowing from his face, he said over and over again, "I forgive you. I forgive you. I forgive you." He then took a cigarette lighter and burned the letter, the ashes falling on his father's grave. For him the ashes symbolized letting go of all the anger and bitterness and hurt. Finally, he got back into his car and drove home. A few days later he told me, "As I drove away from my father's grave, a huge burden was lifted from my soul. I feel a peace I've never felt before."

Forgiveness Principles

God clearly wants us to accept God's forgiveness and then to forgive others. This is at the heart of good faith. Through the years, both from personal experience and from my work as a pastor, I've learned several important lessons about forgiveness. A brief overview follows.

1. *Forgiveness is hard work.* Forgiving other people is a challenge, especially when the infraction is major. Forgiving someone is not easy. It's not natural. It takes discipline and effort. It's worth the effort, but it's not easy.

2. *Forgiveness can take time.* Minor infractions, like the inevitable day-to-day conflicts in marriage and family life, can often be forgiven immediately, without significant effort. But for major infractions, forgiveness can take years. It's a process. It takes time to let go of our hurt and fully forgive.

3. *Forgiveness does not mean we condone bad behavior.* You can fully forgive someone but not accept or condone the behavior, especially in cases of crime or abuse. For example, you can forgive someone for abusing you, but you absolutely do not condone the behavior.

4. *Forgiveness does not always result in reconciliation.* It's beautiful when it does, but that is not always the case. The person we forgive may not acknowledge a need for forgiveness. The person we forgive might be dead. The person we forgive might be dangerous—mentally unstable or even a criminal—and should not be contacted. Forgiving someone does not always repair the relationship.

5. *Forgiveness is primarily for our benefit.* Harboring bitterness, resentment, and anger toward another person deeply damages us—emotionally, spiritually, and even physically. Nelson Mandela was right: resenting and hating others is a prison. In order to be liberated from bitterness we must choose to forgive the person who hurt us and move forward with our life. Ultimately, forgiveness helps us more than it helps the person who is forgiven.

16

⌒⌒

GOOD RELIGION
PROMOTES GRATITUDE

A little over a decade ago, a riveting story made head-lines all over the world. The story involved a young man named Aron Ralston. You may not recognize Aron's name, but you will probably recognize his story. At the time Aron worked as an engineer in Aspen, Colorado. His passion was mountain climbing. In 2003 Aron went on a solo mountain climb in a remote desert canyon in Utah. During his climb Aron had an accident and got his armed pinned under an eight-hundred-pound boulder. He lay there for five days, hoping to be rescued by a search party. But as the days passed by with no rescue, Aron knew he had to do something drastic or he would die. So he took a dull pocketknife out of his pocket and began sawing off his crushed arm. It took two days, but he finally freed himself. Then, with only one arm, he rappelled down a sixty-foot cliff and hiked six miles until he was rescued. Aron made a good recovery and even returned to mountain climbing. A powerful movie was made about his experience in 2010 called *127 Hours*.

Saved by Gratitude

A few months after the incident, I learned that Aron was, at the time of his accident, a member of Hope United Methodist Church in Denver, Colorado. After his amazing experience and recovery, Aron's pastor gave an interview with the media. During the interview this pastor shared Aron's turning point on the mountain, the major factor that empowered him to live rather than die. As Aron lay with his arm stuck under the boulder, he realized that if something didn't change soon, he would not make it. Most people in that situation would be full of fear, dread, despair, or perhaps anger. But not Aron. The overwhelming emotion in his heart was thankfulness. As he lay there, contemplating his impending death, Aron felt overcome with gratitude. He began to remember all the wonderful experiences of his life. He felt thankful for his family. He felt thankful for his friends. He felt thankful for all the hikes he had taken. He felt thankful for the mountains he had climbed. He felt thankful for the sunsets he had witnessed. He felt thankful for all the beautiful music he had enjoyed. Aron felt completely overcome with gratitude for his entire life. At that point he began to think, *I want* more *of that*. And that overwhelming gratitude for life—and the desire for more life—gave Aron the strength to cut off his arm with a pocketknife, rappel down a cliff, and hike to safety. Gratitude literally saved Aron Ralston's life.

Expressing gratitude is a major theme in Scripture. Passages about giving thanks are everywhere in the Bible. For example, Leviticus 22:29 says, "Sacrifice a thank offering to the LORD." First Chronicles 29:13 says, "Now, our God, we give you thanks, and praise your glorious name." Ezra 3:11 says, "With praise and thanksgiving they sang to the LORD." Psalm 95:2 says, "Let us come before him with thanksgiving." Jeremiah 33:11 says, "Give thanks to the LORD Almighty, for the Lord is good; his love endures forever." Matthew, Mark, Luke, and John include multiple examples of Jesus giving thanks. First Corinthians 15:57 says, "But thanks be to God! He gives us the victory through our Lord Jesus Christ." Ephesians 5:20 says, "Always giving thanks to God the Father for everything." And Revelation 11:17 says, "We give thanks to you, Lord God Almighty."

Gratitude is at the heart of religious life. I once heard somebody say, "Gratitude is our most direct line to God." I believe that statement is absolutely correct. Clearly, God wants us to be people of gratitude. One reason God wants us to be thankful is that gratitude is life-giving and healing. Gratitude is good for the soul, good for the heart, good for the mind, and even good for the body. People who are constantly grateful experience far more joy, contentment, and fulfillment than those who are not grateful. God wants us to be thankful because gratitude is a powerful, life-giving practice.

Choosing Gratitude

One of the most important biblical truths about thanksgiving is that gratitude is a choice. A good example can be found in 1 Thessalonians 5:18. In this verse the apostle Paul says, "Give thanks in all circumstances, for this is God's will for you in Christ Jesus." This verse doesn't mean that everything that happens to us is God's will. It's not God's will that we lose our jobs or get a cancer diagnosis, or that our children make poor choices. What this verse does say is that God's will for us is to be thankful people in all circumstances, even in hard times.

This passage reminds me of a scene from the classic novel *Robinson Crusoe*. When Robinson Crusoe was wrecked on his lonely island, he drew two columns and listed the good and bad of his situation. He was cast on a desolate island, but he was still alive. He was divided from humanity, but he was not starving. He had no clothes but was in a warm climate and didn't need them. He had no means of defense but saw no wild beasts to threaten him. He had no one to talk to, but the destroyed ship was near the shore, and he could get out of it all the things necessary for his basic needs. He concluded, therefore, that no condition in the world was so miserable that one could not find something for which to be grateful.

That episode in Robinson Crusoe's life is true for all of us. At any point in our lives, we could draw two columns, a list of good things that are happening to us and a list of bad things that are happening to us. That's just the way life is. And so we have to decide constantly: Will we resent the bad circumstances, or will we be grateful for the good circumstances? Where will our focus be? Resentment or gratitude? It's always our choice.

The apostle Paul chose gratitude not only in his writings but also in his life. Like Robinson Crusoe, Paul could also draw two columns and make a list of good things and bad things. Paul experienced many positive circumstances—starting new churches, reaching many people for Christ, and developing wonderful relationships. But at the same time he also experienced numerous negative circumstances—persecution, physical torture, conflict with other believers, shipwrecks, and imprisonment. In the midst of all these circumstances, good and bad, Paul wrote again and again about thankfulness and gratitude. To the church at Philippi, where he was imprisoned and beaten, he said, "I thank my God every time I remember you" (Phil. 1:3). To the church at Corinth, which caused him all kinds of heartaches and headaches he wrote, "I always thank my God for you" (1 Cor. 1:4). To the church at Ephesus, where he was driven out of town and unjustly accused and persecuted, he wrote, "Always giving thanks to God the Father for everything, in the name of our Lord Jesus Christ" (Eph. 5:20). Paul was no shallow optimist or positive-attitude thinker. He knew the hard realities of suffering. But Paul consistently chose gratitude over resentment, and it had a powerful and positive influence on his life.

Gratitude has great power. It can make a huge difference in our life. It did for John Claypool. When John lost his ten-year-old daughter to leukemia, gratitude was the only way he survived. After his daughter's death John walked down three different paths. The first path was to say, "This must have been God's will. I have to accept it." But that was no good. He could not believe God willed ten-year-old girls to die of leukemia. A second path was to try to find an intellectual answer as to why this happened. He tried to make sense of it, but that didn't work either. His daughter's death did not make any sense at all. Finally, John walked the path of gratitude. He realized that life is a gift. We are not entitled to it. Therefore, he chose to be thankful for the ten good years they had together rather than be consumed with resentment for the years he did not have with her. This path of gratitude wasn't easy, but it was the only path that offered any help. Gratitude saved John's life—spiritually, emotionally, and perhaps even physically.

Gratitude or resentment? It's our choice. And we must make that choice almost every day. Like Robinson Crusoe we can always draw two columns, good and bad. We all have bad things we can be resentful about and good things for which we can be grateful. Therefore, we have to decide where to put the focus—resentment for the bad or gratitude for the good. Although we can choose either one, the Bible is clear. God wants us to choose gratitude. As Paul said, "Give thanks in all circumstances, for this is God's will for you in Christ Jesus" (1 Thess. 5:18). Therefore, good religion constantly encourages the people of God to practice gratitude.

Known by His Gratitude

One of the most famous stories in the Bible is Jesus' post-Easter walk on the Emmaus Road. In this story two of Jesus' followers are walking down the road from Jerusalem to Emmaus. It's afternoon on Easter Sunday. As they walked on the road, Jesus joined them. At first they did not recognize him. Why? Many theories exist. But regardless of the reason, they did not know it was Jesus. As the three of them walked down the road, they engaged in a long conservation. Finally, when they got to Emmaus, the two men invited Jesus for dinner. Before they ate, they asked Jesus to say grace over the meal. He took bread, broke it, gave thanks to God, and handed it to them. And when he did, their eyes were opened. The light came on. They realized it was Jesus. In short, they recognized Jesus by his gratitude. When he lifted the bread to heaven and thanked God, that's when they knew it was Jesus.

Jesus was recognized by his gratitude. And that gratitude was not a onetime deal. Throughout his entire ministry Jesus exhibited a grateful spirit. He gave thanks to God for every good gift. In many ways gratitude defined him.

Through the years I've known numerous people whose primary characteristic is gratitude. That was true of my grandfather. What I most remember about him was his overwhelming thankfulness for the gifts of life. My granddad had little in terms of material wealth. He lived almost all his life in a small frame house. He worked forty years as a meter reader for the gas company. He had no social status in town. He wasn't a member of the country club or Rotary Club or chamber of commerce. And yet he was the most grateful man I've ever known. I remember Sunday lunches at his home. Before we ate, he always said grace. In that prayer he thanked God for the food, for his family, for his church, for his friends, and for Jesus. And it was always a *sincere* prayer. He expressed gratitude for every gift of life, no matter how small or simple.

My most vivid memory of my granddad is the funeral service for his wife, my grandmother. They had been married over fifty years. When the service was over, everyone left the church except the family. My granddad stood over the casket, weeping in grief. But in spite of his overwhelming grief, he offered a remarkable prayer. He said, "Lord, thank you for my wonderful wife. Thank you for the fifty years we had together. Thank you for her love. Thank you for the children you blessed us with." Here he was, in overwhelming pain and grief, and yet he was full of thanksgiving. He was, like Jesus, known by others for his gratitude.

Jesus was known by his gratitude. We would do well to follow his example and live a life of constant thanksgiving. In fact, it would be a worthy goal to practice thankfulness so much that we, like Jesus, are known by our gratitude.

A few months ago I read an article about a United Methodist minister in Arkansas who recently retired. The article included a section called "Self-Portrait." In this section the retired pastor answered several questions including, what was his favorite book, what was the best advice he ever got, what was his pet peeve, and what he was most looking forward to in retirement. The last question was, "What one word would sum you up?" His answer was, "Thankful."

17

GOOD RELIGION PRACTICES EVANGELISM WITH INTEGRITY

Many years ago, when Fred Craddock graduated from seminary, he pastored a small church in Oak Ridge, Tennessee. It was a beautiful little white church up on a hill. At that time Oak Ridge was rapidly expanding. Lots of people moved to town to help in construction work. Many of the newcomers lived in a mobile home park located near the church. The trailer park swarmed with newcomers, including a large number of children. Fred saw all those new people and thought, *Our church ought to reach out to them.* So at the next board meeting Fred recommended a plan to reach out to the newcomers.

"Oh, I don't know," said the chairman of the board. "They might not fit in here very well."

Fred said, "But they live right next to our church. I think we should invite them to worship with us." But Fred's idea met with resistance. They finally decided to table the discussion and deal with it at their next business meeting.

At that meeting a leader of the congregation said, "I move that in order to be a member of this church, you have to own property in the county."

"I'll second that motion," said another man. Fred was mortified and passionately spoke against it. But in the end the motion passed. As a result, no effort was ever made to reach out to the newcomers. Soon thereafter Fred left that church.

Twenty years later Fred and his wife drove past Oak Ridge on a trip through Tennessee. Since he was single when he served that church, his wife had never seen it. So Fred decided to show it to her. As they drove to the church, Fred told his wife that painful story of how the congregation refused to reach out to newcomers in the community. It took a while to find the church. Lots of new roads and homes had been built in the area, but they finally found the spot. The beautiful white-frame church sat on the hill as always, but something seemed different. Out front stood a big parking lot full of cars, trucks, motor homes, and even motorcycles. As they pulled into the lot, they saw a big sign in front of the church. It said, "BBQ: All You Can Eat." The old church had been converted into a restaurant! Fred and his wife walked inside, and the place was packed with all kinds of people. White and black and Hispanic. Rich and poor. Southerners and northerners. Fred said to his wife, "It's a good thing this isn't a church anymore. If it were, these people would not be allowed in."

The Son of Man Came to Seek and to Save the Lost

That's a sad story, but it happens a lot. Many churches, especially mainline churches, do not practice evangelism. They don't invite new people to their church; when guests do come, they are not welcomed warmly, especially if the guests are different from the congregation. The end result is stagnation, decline, and, eventually, death. But the Bible is clear. God expects the church of Jesus Christ to invite and welcome all people. We see that in Jesus' parable in Luke 14 where the master says, "Go out quickly into the streets and alleys of the town and bring in the poor, the crippled, the blind and the lame. . . . Go out to the roads and country lanes and compel them to come in, so that my house will be full" (vv. 21, 23).

Reaching people was a huge priority for Jesus. He once said, "The Son of Man came to seek and to save the lost" (Luke 19:10). That is an important passage of Scripture. Jesus said his primary mission in life was to reach lost people. Jesus once told a story about a shepherd with one hundred sheep. One got lost, so he left the ninety-nine to find the lost one and rejoiced when he found it. In his last words to his disciples, he said, "Therefore go and make disciples of all nations" (Matt. 28:19). More than anything, Jesus wanted people to be connected to God. He said to his disciples, "The harvest is plentiful but the workers are few" (Matt. 9:37). Jesus said many people out there can be reached. We just need to reach them.

Some churches, like Fred Craddock's in Tennessee, resist evangelism because they don't want new people to attend their church, especially people different from them. But that's not the norm. Most churches really do want to reach people. But many don't. Why? I think most mainline churches avoid evangelism because they have been turned off by pushy, manipulative, annoying evangelism tactics.

The Burning Hell

Many years ago, when I pastored a Baptist church in Arkansas, churches all over the state were showing a film called *The Burning Hell.* It depicted life in hell, full of fire and screaming and worms coming out of people's eyes. The film was followed by a heavy-handed invitation, and hundreds of little children from across the state came flocking down the aisle to be saved. I saw the film at a neighboring church and felt so disgusted by this manipulative abuse of children that it made me physically ill.

A few days later a sponsor of the film called me and said, "Reverend Thielen, when can we schedule *The Burning Hell* for your church?"

I said, "You can't." But he persisted. He went on and on about how great an evangelistic tool the film was, and surely I didn't want to be left out. I'm a pretty diplomatic guy, but I finally lost my cool. I told the man that "hell would freeze over before I showed that film in my church," and that pretty well ended the conversation.

Through the years I've had a lot of bad experiences with evangelism. Long and manipulative altar calls. High-pressure gospel presentations. Annoying people on street corners who hand out religious tracts. Manipulative invitations at funerals of children and teenagers. I finally decided that if this is evangelism, then I wanted no part of it. So for about a year I just gave up on it. In time, however, I realized that my problem was not with evangelism but with inappropriate methods of evangelism. I came to realize that evangelism—reaching people for Christ and church—was at the heart of the gospel. Since that time my goal has been to do evangelism—but evangelism with integrity. The fact is, Christians and churches *can* do evangelism with integrity. Let me review three ways we can do this.

First, Christians and churches can engage in *life-style evangelism.* One of the best ways we can witness to our faith is to live it. As Jesus said in the Sermon on the Mount, "Let your light shine before others, that they may see your good deeds and glorify your Father in heaven" (Matt.

5:16). When we live like Christ—when we live lives of love, grace, compassion, integrity, service, and social justice—we testify that we are people of faith. People see our lives and think, "If this is what Christianity looks like, I'm interested." Francis of Assisi once said, "Preach the gospel at all times. Use words if necessary." This is life-style evangelism, and God calls all of us to do it.

Second, Christians and churches can engage in *relational evangelism*. We need to live like Christians, but we also need to share our faith verbally. I'm not talking about a sales pitch or pressuring people or annoying them. But all of us, in our network of relationships, can find opportunities to share our faith naturally with people we know. It can be as simple as letting folks know that our faith is important to us, grounds us, gives us meaning and purpose, helps us through hard times, and motivates us to serve others. We see this spirit in 1 Peter 3:15. In this text Peter says, "Always be prepared to give an answer to everyone who asks you to give the reason for the hope that you have. But do this with gentleness and respect." God wants us to find verbal ways to share our faith with the people in our life. This kind of relational evangelism can be done naturally in our conversations with others and can make a huge impact on people.

Third, Christians and churches can engage in *invitational evangelism*. In short, this is a "come-and-see" method of evangelism. The most common form of invitational witness is to invite people to church for worship or a special event or to a small group. This is a simple, easy, and exceptionally effective way to share faith. Studies constantly show that about 90 percent of people first visit a church because somebody they know invited them to come. We see this approach in John 1. In this passage Andrew invited Simon to come and see Jesus. Then Philip invited Nathanael to come and see Jesus. We obviously can't invite people to come and see Jesus. But we can invite people to come and see the church of Jesus Christ. If we do, many will come, and through that experience they can come to know Jesus.

The Informer

Harvey Cox once told a story about a Baptist church in the Northeast. One Sunday a Hispanic man showed up. Nobody knew who he was. But he kept coming back, and eventually he joined the church. He told them he was from El Salvador and had recently immigrated to this country. About a year later they found out this was not entirely true. He confided that he had actually come to the United States illegally, and now Immigration Services was after him. In fact, they planned to deport him back to El Salvador. He told the church that if that happened, he would be killed upon his return.

The church didn't know what to do. They didn't approve of breaking the law. But he was a member of their church. So they gulped hard and made a momentous decision. They put a cot in the basement of the church, moved him in, and told Immigration Services that their church was a sanctuary, and they must not come in and take him away. Immigration authorities didn't have to honor that, but they didn't want any trouble with a church, so they reported the situation to the FBI. The FBI decided to place an informer in the congregation, and the church soon found out. They didn't know who the informer was. They just knew that out there on Sunday morning, somebody praying the prayers and singing the hymns was a spy.

A lot of people in the congregation were amused. They said, "You don't have to put an informer in this church to find out what's going on. This is a Baptist church, for goodness sake! We know more about one another than we ought to know." But others in the congregation were nervous. Several months later, during a Sunday morning worship service, the pastor prayed the morning prayer. He prayed for the lost and for the sick, and then he said, "Lord, we ask a special blessing today on our informer."

Harvey Cox, who wrote this story, added a commentary. He said, "I'm so glad that pastor prayed for the informer. And I hope the informer will not grow weary and go away. Who knows, if he sings 'Amazing Grace' enough times, he may end up being saved. It wouldn't be the first time."

Harvey Cox knew that, under the influence of the church, even an FBI informer could be touched by God. When people come to church, something mysterious begins to happen. The Holy Spirit begins to work on their hearts. As they meet loving Christian people, pray the prayers, sing the songs, hear the gospel, and take Communion, God does a work in their life. I see that happen all the time. People tell me on a regular basis, "I visited this church and found God in this place." Invitational evangelism is easy. We simply invite people to visit our church, welcome them, and leave the rest to God.

Reaching people for Christ and church is one of the most important things we can do as Christians. Why? Because Jesus commanded us to do so. And because people, more than anything else, need to know Jesus and to be a part of the body of Christ.

Welcome to Our Church

I once heard a story about a young college student named Bill. Bill had wild hair, spiked with vivid colors, and he wore a nose ring. Bill always wore a T-shirt with holes in it, blue jeans, and no shoes. Bill, a brilliant young man, became a Christian while attending college. He attended a Christian organization on campus, but he also wanted to find a church. Across the street from Bill's college sat a well-dressed, traditional church.

One Sunday Bill decided to visit that church. He walked into the sanctuary with his nose ring, no shoes, jeans and a T-shirt, and wild hair. The service had already started, so Bill walked down the aisle looking for a seat. But the church was packed, and he could not find a seat anywhere. By now people were uncomfortable, but no one said anything. Bill got closer to the front of the church. When he realized there were no seats left, he squatted down and sat in the aisle. Although this was perfectly acceptable behavior at his college fellowship group—trust me—this had never happened before in this church! The tension in the congregation was palpable. The preacher didn't know what to do, so he stood there in silence.

About that time an elderly man, one of the old patriarchs of that church, slowly made his way down the aisle toward Bill. The man, in his eighties, had silver-gray hair and always wore a three-piece suit. He was a godly man— elegant, dignified, traditional, and conservative. As he started walking toward this boy, everyone was saying to themselves, *You can't blame him for what he's going to do. How can you expect a man of his age and of his background to understand some college kid with a nose ring, wild hair, T-shirt and jeans and no shoes, sitting on the church floor?* They knew he would banish this kid from the church. The old man walked with a cane, so it took a long time for him to reach the boy. The church was utterly silent except for the clicking of the old man's cane. All eyes focused on him. Finally the old man reached the boy. He paused a moment and then dropped his cane on the floor. With great difficulty the old man lowered himself and sat down next to the boy. He shook the boy's hand, said, "Welcome to our church," and sat with him for the rest of the service.

Other Examples of Good Religion

Many other examples of good religion could be discussed, including the following:

— Good (Christian) religion is Christ-centered. For an overview of Christ's life, teachings, example, death, and resurrection, see my previous book, *What's the Least I Can Believe and Still Be a Christian? A Guide to What Matters Most.*
— Good religion is inclusive.
— Good religion supports equality between men and women.
— Good religion fights for human rights of all kinds.
— Good religion inspires awe and mystery before God.
— Good religion gives people strength, comfort, and resiliency in life's struggles.
— Good religion, while affirming the ancient message of faith, is willing to communicate and live out that message with creative new methods of ministry.

CONCLUSION

Although we've discussed many important topics in this book, at heart, three core affirmations have been made. First, bad religion—unfortunately—abounds in today's world. Second, the fact that bad religion exists is no reason to jettison religion altogether. Third, the best answer to bad religion is to practice good religion.

The truth of these three affirmations can be seen in the experience of the Walker family mentioned in the preface. For many years, the Walkers looked at the narrow-minded, negative, and judgmental religion around them and said, "If this is Christianity, we don't want any part of it." However, deep in their soul, they longed for a connection with God and a community of faith. So they took a risk and explored mainline faith, hoping to find a viable alternative to Christian fundamentalism. When they did, they discovered, like millions of others, that the answer to bad religion is not no religion but good religion. When I think about the Walker family, my prayer is simple: "Lord, may their tribe increase!"

It's been a joy to share these thoughts about good religion with you. If you found this book helpful, I hope you'll give a copy to a friend or family member, especially someone who has been turned off by bad religion. If you attend a church, you might find it beneficial to study this book with other people in your congregation. Information about how to do that can be found on the following page. If you don't attend a church, I strongly encourage you to find one that proclaims and practices good religion. Connecting with such a congregation is one of the most life-giving experiences you can have. I'd suggest looking for a congregation in the mainline or moderate tradition. Examples include United Methodist, Presbyterian, Lutheran, Episcopal, Disciples of Christ, United Church of Christ, American Baptist, Cooperative Baptist, or the Alliance of Baptists. Although no congregation is perfect, many of them are committed to living out good religion. They would love to have you join them on their journey.

APPENDIX 1

ADDITIONAL RESOURCES

Several additional resources are available to help you and your congregation study this book. These include

— a six-week leader's guide, *The Answer to Bad Religion Is Not No Religion—Leader's Guide* (ISBN 978-0-664-25960-0)
— an outreach and worship kit, available on a flash drive, complete with sermon ideas, prayers, hymn and song suggestions, suggestions for publicizing the study, and graphics (ISBN 978-0-664-25961-7)
— the author's previous book, *What's the Least I Can Believe and Still Be a Christian? A Guide to What Matters Most* (ISBN 978-0664-23938-1)
— the author's website, www.GettingReadyforSunday .com. Here you will find preaching, worship, and pastoral leadership articles, sermons and sermon series, and other helpful information.

APPENDIX 2

TAKING THE BIBLE SERIOUSLY BUT NOT ALWAYS LITERALLY

"O daughter Babylon, you devastor! Happy shall they be who pay you back what you have done to us! Happy shall they be who take your little ones and dash them against the rock!"

— Psalm 137:8-9

Many centuries ago a bald holy man walked down a road on his way to the city. As he neared the city, he came upon a group of boys. When the boys saw his bald head, they began to tease him, saying, "Go away, Baldhead! Go away, Baldhead!" In anger the holy man called down God's curse upon the little boys. Immediately, two vicious bears emerged from the woods and mauled them. Unfazed by the screaming, violence, and blood from the bears ripping the little boys' bodies apart, the holy man continued his journey into the city.

Where does that awful story come from? It comes from the story of the prophet Elisha in the holy Bible (2 Kgs. 2:23–25). And there are plenty more biblical texts just like it, including the vengeful passage listed above from Psalm 137. In this text the psalmist, full of hatred for the Babylonians, wants to murder Babylonian infants by smashing their little bodies against the rocks.

Somewhere along the way, Christian believers must answer a crucial question about these kinds of troubling texts, which are so prevalent in the Bible. Are such passages meant to be taken literally? Does God really send bears from the woods to rip apart little boys for teasing a prophet? Or was this a campfire story the ancient Israelites told their children and grandchildren to engender respect for the holy prophets of Israel? How you answer that question will have a huge impact on how you understand Christian faith. Ultimately it will determine if you fall into the literalist, fundamentalist camp of Christianity or the mainline and moderate camp.

People hold one of three positions about biblical inspiration. People believe that the Bible is either (1) all human, (2) all divine, or (3) both human and divine. Let's review all three.

The Bible is all human. This position says the Bible is inspired, but no more so than Shakespeare or any other great work of literature. However, this is not a viable option for Christian believers who consider the Bible to be "the Word of God for the people of God." From the very beginning, Christians have affirmed that the Bible is "Holy Scripture." Although Christians hold differing views of biblical inspiration, as we'll see below, virtually all Christian believers and churches affirm that the Bible is divinely inspired. As a result, Christians hold the Bible in high esteem, turning to it for both doctrinal beliefs and behavioral guidance. Therefore, for the vast majority of Christians, an all-human Bible is not an acceptable option.

The Bible is all divine. This position says that everything in the Bible is literal, including all historic, geographical,

and scientific details. Although this view is held by fundamentalist churches, it's not the historic Christian position.
In fact, this view of the Bible, called "biblical inerrancy," is
quite new in Christian history. It first appeared in the early
1900s in reaction to modern science (especially the theory
of evolution) and modern biblical scholarship (called "the
historical-critical method"). Conservative believers felt
threatened by these modern views, so they adopted the
concept of an "inerrant and infallible" Bible that could not
be questioned by modern science or scholarship. Unfortunately, this view of Scripture is overwhelmingly problem-
atic. For example, if everything in the Bible is literal, then

— The earth is flat.
— Creation took place six thousand years ago.
— The world was created in six, twenty-four-hour days.
— Women are the property of men.
— Slavery is approved by God.
— Polygamy is approved by God.
— In order to win a bet with the devil, God let Satan
  kill all ten of Job's children.
— God throws raging, jealous, violent fits, killing thou-
  sands in the process.
— Eating shellfish is an abomination to God.
— Wearing blended garments (like cotton/polyester)
  enrages God.
— Menstruating women and handicapped men are not
  allowed in public worship.
— God's preferred system of government is a mon-
  archy.
— All governments, even highly oppressive ones, are
  established by God.
— God approves of genocide and commanded people
  to practice it.
— Women are to be silent in church.

— Women are to wear veils in church.
— People who commit adultery should be stoned to death.
— The penalty for working on the Sabbath is execution.
— Sassy teenagers are to be executed.

The above examples are just a few of the massive problems that come with biblical inerrancy. For example, if the Bible is all divine, how do you explain its inconsistencies? In the book of Matthew, we are told that Judas, the disciple who betrayed Jesus, hanged himself. However, in the book of Acts, we are told that Judas fell down in a field and died from massive internal rupturing of his organs. Both stories can't be true. So why do we have two conflicting stories in Scripture about the death of Judas? The answer is simple. When the Bible was written—many decades after the original events occurred—two different stories were circulating about Judas's death. The writer of Matthew picked up one story, and the writer of Acts picked up the other. If space permitted, hundreds of examples of inconsistencies in the Bible could be given, including conflicting accounts of the birth and resurrection of Christ.

Another example of the problems that come with biblical literalism can be found in the familiar story of Noah and the ark in Genesis 6–8. Although many people believe that the Noah story literally happened, a lot of sincere and thoughtful Christians are reluctant, for several reasons, to affirm a literal reading of the text. First, no scientific evidence exists to suggest that the earth ever experienced a worldwide flood. Major floods have occurred locally and regionally, but it's doubtful that the entire earth ever flooded. Also, how is it possible that every species on the planet was placed into one boat, even a big one? From a scientific analysis, the story has overwhelming problems.

Second, the Genesis flood story is extremely similar to an ancient Babylonian myth that predates the Bible. Even a casual reading of the two stories leads to the likely conclusion that the Israelites borrowed the ancient story, adapted it, and retold it according to their purposes. Finally, significant theological challenges exist with the passage. If the Noah story literally happened, then God purposely annihilated every living creature on the earth in a worldwide genocidal flood. This image of God is hard to reconcile with Jesus' teachings that God is like a heavenly Father who deeply loves his children, even sinful ones like the prodigal son. Valuable theological lessons can be found in the story of Noah, including the fact that God takes sin seriously and God expects us, like Noah, to live righteous and faithful lives in a pagan culture. But one can affirm these theological truths without believing in a literal, worldwide, genocidal flood.

Many years ago I had a conversation about biblical literalism with an extremely conservative pastor. We were talking about the Old Testament stories of David killing his archenemies, the Philistines. Several of those stories claim that David single-handedly killed hundreds of Philistines at a time. I said to this pastor, "What if the biblical writers exaggerated the number of Philistines that David killed in any given battle? What if he killed only thirty instead of three hundred? Would that matter?" The pastor replied, "If that were true, I would have to quit the ministry and renounce my faith. If I can't believe everything in the Bible, then I can't believe anything in the Bible." Sadly, this kind of radical literalism is extremely damaging to the Christian faith. It forces people to take an all-or-nothing approach to Scripture, a totally unnecessary choice that the Bible does not require.

For these and many other reasons, the vast majority of Christian believers do not affirm biblical inerrancy. And they don't need to affirm or accept it. Only a small percentage of Christians advocate this position. The Bible itself never claims to be inerrant; it claims only to be inspired. Biblical inerrancy has never been the historic position of the church. In fact, the church existed for nineteen centuries *without* this view. Belief in biblical inerrancy is not necessary for Christians and is, in fact, detrimental to authentic faith. Telling people they must believe something that intellectual and theological integrity cannot authentically accept only hurts the Christian cause. Thankfully, a third and far more promising position exists concerning biblical inspiration.

The Bible is both human and divine. This is the classic position of the church, held by virtually all mainline and moderate denominations. This view states that the Bible was inspired by God. People who hold this position affirm, along with the Bible, that "all Scripture is God-breathed and is useful for teaching, rebuking, correcting and training in righteousness" (2 Tim. 3:16 NIV). The Christian church has always affirmed that God inspired the Bible, that Holy Scripture has a divine element. But the church also affirms that the Bible is a *human* document. People, not God, wrote the Bible. And they wrote it according to the worldview of their time, which was a prescientific world. For example, the biblical writers believed that the world was flat and that mental illness was caused by demons. Those kinds of prescientific views are reflected throughout the Bible.

A concrete example of human involvement in the Bible is found in Luke 1. Luke begins his Gospel by writing, "Therefore, since I have carefully investigated everything from the beginning, it seemed good also to me to write an orderly account" (1:3 NIV). We clearly see human involvement here. Luke did his homework. He researched his subject well and eventually wrote the Gospel of Luke and the book of Acts. Although God inspired Luke's writing, Luke was fully involved in the process. In short, Luke's Gospel is the product of divine inspiration as well as human insight and human limitations.

Clearly Christians do not have to interpret everything in the Bible literally. In fact, since some passages of Scripture express pre-Christian and even sub-Christian views of God, Christians *should not* interpret everything literally. However, that does *not* mean the Bible is not true. For example, take the first book of the Bible. Genesis is full of many great truths: God created the world, human beings are created in God's image, human sin is real, and God dearly loves all creation. However, a person can believe these great truths without believing that the earth is flat, that the world is only six thousand years old, that serpents talk to people, or that Noah literally placed two representatives of every living creature on earth into one boat.

I love the Bible. My life has been transformed by the message of the Bible. I believe that the Bible is true and trustworthy and reliable. I affirm the great truths of the Bible. For example, I believe God created the world. I believe God called Abraham and Sarah to give birth to a nation through whom God blessed the world. I believe the Ten Commandments and the prophet's demands for justice. I believe the Great Commandment, the Great Commission, and the Golden Rule. And most important, I believe, as the Bible teaches, in the life, death, and bodily resurrection of Jesus Christ. However, like most Christians through most of Christian history, I do not believe that everything in the Bible has to be understood literally.

Christians must always remember that we worship God, not the Bible. The Bible *points* us to God, but the Bible is *not* God. Many years ago John the Baptist came upon the scene, preparing the way for Jesus. When people went to hear John preach, they asked him, "Are you the Messiah?"

John said, "No, I am not the Messiah, but I bear witness to the Messiah." The same is true for the Bible. The Bible is not God, but the Bible bears witness to God. Therefore, Holy Scripture is central to our faith.